The right tool for the job

Open your image, identify the jobs that need doing, and, after putting the kettle on, have a good old rummage through Photoshop's toolbox

Photoshop is all about tools. Tools for correcting the exposure of your images, tools for editing colour, tools for selecting specific areas of a shot, and tools that enable you to perform all manner of other image-editing tasks. Many of these tools are, not surprisingly, found in Photoshop's toolbox – The Brush Tool and Magnetic Lasso Tool, for example, and some have their origins in traditional darkroom processes, such as the Dodge and Burn tools. Other tools are found in Photoshop's extensive system of menus and palettes, and are more accurately described as commands or dialogs.

In this Focus Guide we'll show you how to use these tools to maximum effect to diagnose and correct problems with your images, to enhance them, and to transform them in more unusual and creative ways. If you're fairly new to Photoshop we'll start with the basics, and if you're a more experienced user we'll show you how to use familiar tools in new ways, and how to configure their advanced settings to unleash their full power.

You'll learn how to correct exposure problems using professional tools such as Levels and Curves, as well as 'one-click' alternatives, and we'll also show you how to correct the colours in your images, and change them completely if you so wish. You'll discover how to clone, transplant and transform pixels as we blur the line between editing and image manipulation, and we'll show you how you can keep your options open, and edit images non-destructively, by using adjustment layers and layer masks.

We've also featured several of the unique tools in Photoshop CS2, such as the amazing Vanishing Point filter, which enables you to clone and paste pixels in perspective. If you're using Elements you don't have quite the same selection of tools, although all the important ones are there, and where tools are accessed in different ways, or you need to use a different technique to perform a particular task, we'll let you know. So roll up your sleeves, turn the page, and clock-in for a shift at the image-editing workshop…

Future Publishing Ltd
30 Monmouth Street, Bath BA1 2BW, UK
www.futurenet.co.uk
Tel +44 (0)1225 44 22 44 Fax +44 (0)1225 44 60 19

Writer	**George Cairns**
Editor	**Alex Summersby**
	digitalbookazines@futurenet.co.uk
Production Editor	**Mike McNally**
Art Editor	**Christy Walters**
New Media Editor	**Becky Collier**
Senior Editor	**Paul Newman**
Senior Art Editor	**Richard Llewellyn**
New Media Co-ordinator	**Trevor Witt**
Production Co-ordinator	**Mark Anson**
Marketing Manager	**Fiona Tully**
Publisher	**Kelley Corten**
Publishing Director	**Dom Beaven**

Cover Image: Photolibrary.com

Distributed through the UK Newstrade by
Marketforce (UK) Ltd, 5th Floor, Low Rise Building,
Kings Reach Tower, Stamford Street, London, SE1 9LS
Overseas Distribution by **Future Publishing Ltd.**

SUBSCRIPTIONS & BACK ISSUES

If you have a query regarding a subscription or back issue, or would like
to place an order, please contact our customer services team:
Telephone: +44 (0)870 837 4722
Email: customerservice@futurenet.co.uk
www.myfavouritemagazines.co.uk

Printed in the EU

All contents © 2006 Future Publishing Ltd

Future Publishing is part of Future plc.

Future plc produces carefully targeted specialist magazines for people who share a
passion. We aim to satisfy that passion by creating titles which offer value for money,
reliable information, and smart buying advice and which are a pleasure to read.
Today we publish more than 100 magazines in the UK, US, France and Italy. Over
100 international editions of our magazines are also published in 30 other countries
across the world. Future plc is a public company quoted on the London Stock
Exchange (symbol: FUTR).

Non-executive Chairman	Roger Parry
Chief Executive	Stevie Spring
Group Finance Director	John Bowman

Tel +44 (0)1225 442244 www.futureplc.com

Bath • London • Milan • New York • Paris • San Francisco

We recommend that you always maintain an
up-to-date backup of your hard disk data.
Future Publishing does not accept any responsibility
for disruption, damage and/or loss to your data or
computer system that may occur while carrying out
procedures described in this publication.

Finding your way

Our handy icons hold the key to a wealth of additional information, both in your Focus Guide and on the disc

Where do you start? With so much to tell you about getting the most out of the tools in Photoshop and Elements it's difficult to find enough room for all the information we want to pack in, and that's why you'll find the sidebars that occupy the margins on each page so useful.

As you leaf through the pages, you'll notice that these sidebars are headed by a range of eye-catching symbols, to help you to identify exactly what kind of information

you're dealing with – for a guide to icon categories, see below. These hints and tips are always relevant to the topic that's being discussed, and will help you master all the tools and techniques that little bit faster.

Our writers are all experienced Photoshop experts who regularly contribute to our sister magazines, such as *Computer Arts* and *Digital Camera Magazine*, so you can rest assured that all the information they provide is both authoritative and thoroughly tried and tested.

On your CD
Trial software, tutorial files, a PDF version of our issue 24 'Brushes & Painting' Focus Guide and more are included on your CD. Every now and then we remind you of this by flagging up the disc icon, and listing the relevant disc contents for that page.

Top tips
This indicates an expert tip. Anything sheltered beneath this icon is guaranteed to reveal a useful tip or advice about Adobe Photoshop's or Photoshop Elements' range of tools, options and features.

Further information
This icon indicates additional information that complements the main text on the page. We may also refer you to other useful resources – such as websites and specialist books – for further reading.

Shortcuts
Carrying out common tasks again and again can get a little tedious. Our handy shortcuts show you how to perform these tasks with a few deft key-presses, saving you lots of time and effort.

Take note
You'll find these nuggets of knowledge scattered throughout every Focus Guide. Every one contains useful information that you should bear in mind while reading or following the instructions on that page.

Watch out!
The 'skull and crossbones' sign means that you should proceed with caution. You'll find some important points outlined below this icon, which you should certainly take seriously.

Links
When we refer to a website, we may pull out the web address in the sidebar to make it easier for you to read and remember.

Photoshop version
Where there are differences in the way that Photoshop Elements, or older versions of Photoshop, handle particular tasks, or if certain tools are located in different places in the interface, this icon will alert you.

CONTENTS

Customising Photoshop

CREATING YOUR IMAGE-EDITING WORKSPACE 10

Before you begin editing images in Photoshop it's worth taking a little time to ensure that both your physical and virtual work areas are set up so you can operate effectively

Colour editing

CORRECTING AND ENHANCING YOUR COLOURS 22

Photoshop boasts a variety of tools that will enable you to restore an image's true colours quickly and effectively, and in this chapter we'll show you how to get the best out of them

Contents

Tonal adjustments

CORRECTING EXPOSURE PROBLEMS   40

Photoshop has a variety of tools to help you correct the tonal range of your images. We'll show you how to use them to produce images with strong contrast and maximum detail

The selection tools

CREATING AND MODIFYING SELECTIONS   62

You can use a number of different tools to isolate specific pixels in an image for editing. We'll explain which tool to use, and show you how you can quickly create perfect selections

Contents

Image manipulation

MASTER THE CLONING AND HEALING TOOLS   88

Photoshop's powerful cloning tools enable you to alter your images in all kinds of ways, from quickly covering up minor blemishes to removing a person from a shot altogether!

Correcting noise and distortion

REMOVING CAMERA ARTIFACTS   100

As well as failing to capture colour and contrast accurately, your camera can introduce artifacts such as chromatic aberration and lens distortion. In this chapter we'll show you how to fix them

Contents

Creative project

PUTTING YOUR EDITING SKILLS INTO PRACTICE 110

We'll finish off by using many of the tools and techniques covered in this guide to edit some typical wedding photos, and create a stylish cover for a DVD photo album or slide show

Essential Information

CD PAGES AND RESOURCES 122

Your essential guide to the software on your CD – plus our handy glossary and details of what essential Photoshop trickery you can look forward to in next month's packed issue

CREATING YOUR IMAGE-EDITING WORKSPACE

Before you begin editing images in Photoshop it's worth taking a little time to ensure that both your physical and virtual work areas are set up so you can operate effectively

Most of the tools that you use around the house come with instructions to show you how to use them safely and effectively. For example, stepladders have stickers on their sides warning you not to use them on uneven floors; advice like this is certainly worth heeding or you could come a cropper the next time you climb into the loft to store your junk!

The comfort zone

Although Photoshop's tools are very unlikely to cause you physical injury (you can't drop a virtual tool on your foot, after all!), there is a physical aspect to consider when you're editing images in Photoshop. You may well spend countless hours touching-up your digital photos, and if you're not sitting correctly you risk long-term back pain and other problems. In this opening chapter we'll show you how to set up your physical workspace so that you can work comfortably, safely and productively. We'll also explain why you need to consider some other environmental factors, including lighting and even the colour scheme of the area in which you work, both of which can have a bearing on how you perceive colours on your screen. You'll find that time spend on such non-Photoshop matters will enable

Page 13 *Calibrate your monitor so that printed colours match those on-screen*

Page 15 *Streamline Photoshop's interface to speed up your workflow*

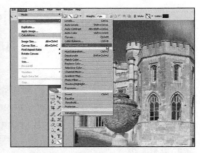

Page 16 *Use colour-coded menus to help you find the right tools for any job*

Page 17 *Create a leaner menu system by hiding the options you don't use*

Page 19 *Fine-tune the way in which certain tools and commands work*

Page 20 *Customise your tool cursors so you can work with greater accuracy*

you to work more efficiently when you launch the program itself.

Lean and mean

When you do launch Photoshop the first thing you need to do is calibrate your monitor so that you can be confident you're seeing an accurate representation of your images' tonal range and colours; we'll show you how to do this on both a PC and a Mac. Then we'll show you how to set up your Photoshop workspace so that you can access the tools you use most often without being distracted by the less-relevant palettes and menus. You'll learn how to create a leaner interface so that you can

quickly grab the right tool for any job without having to wade through menus, palettes or the toolbox.

Once you're sitting comfortably, and have a workspace customised to your specific needs, you'll be able to get down to work. Photoshop is an extremely versatile package, and as such it offers several different options for doing most jobs. In the following chapters we'll demonstrate the strengths and weaknesses of each tool and command so that you'll be able to decide which works best for you, and with a little practice you'll soon find that you're able to select the right tool for any image-editing challenge, and use it effectively.

The physical workspace

Organise your working environment so that you can operate comfortably and effectively

Monitor stands
To adjust the height of your monitor so that the top of the screen is directly in front of your eye line, you can place it on a stand or even mount it on a flexible arm for easier adjustment. Visit www.ergomounts.co.uk for a comprehensive selection of flexible mounts and adjustable stands.

Before you embark on a major image-editing session it's well worth spending a little time thinking about how your working environment affects the way you perceive your images on-screen. Several factors can make it harder to perform accurate adjustments, especially when you're tweaking colours. Your desk may be positioned near a window where, as well as causing distracting glare and reflections on your monitor, natural light coming through a window has a different colour temperature (see sidebar)

at different times of the day and in different weather conditions. Varying light can cause you to perceive the colours and tonal range of your images incorrectly, and could cause you to make a mistake when trying to remove a colour cast, for example. Close the curtains, and use daylight temperature bulbs of 5,000K to produce well-balanced and consistent lighting: this will enable you to edit your images more effectively and accurately, without being confused by lighting that's too warm (orange) or too cold (blue).

Colour temperature
Different light sources have different colour temperatures, which are measured in degrees Kelvin (K). Indoor light from tungsten bulbs has a colour temperature of around 3,200K, and is much warmer (more orange) than cooler (bluer) outdoor light, which has a colour temperature of 5,000-6,000K. Differing colour temperatures can cause all sorts of colour-related problems when you're taking and editing photos, as we'll see in the next chapter.

ARE YOU SITTING COMFORTABLY?

☐ **YOUR MONITOR SHOULD** be at arm's length from your eyes. Give your eyes a break from operating at a fixed focal length for extended periods of time by focusing on objects in the distance now and again.

☐ **PLACE THE MONITOR** directly in front of you, and adjust its height until your eyes are in line with the top of the screen and your neck is in a neutral position, so you don't have to move your head up or down.

☐ **INVEST IN A CHAIR** that you can adjust so that your feet are on the ground and your knees are level with your hips. Your elbows should be at desk height. Splashing out on an ergonomically designed chair could help you avoid posture-related problems in the future.

☐ **SITTING IN THE SAME POSITION** for hours on end can lead to aches and pains as well as eye strain. Take regular breaks and make yourself a cup of tea (or treat the dog to an extra walk!).

Accurate colours

Make sure the colours that come out of your printer match those you see on your screen

Before you start editing your images make sure that your monitor is showing you an accurate representation of their colours and tones. What you see on-screen is not always what you'll get when it comes to viewing your pictures in print (or on another monitor). Details in a shot's darkest shadows may be visible on-screen, but may be lost when the image is printed, for example. If your monitor is too dark you may think that your pictures are also too dark, causing you to lighten them unnecessarily to compensate.

Incorrect contrast settings on your monitor can lead you to lighten or darken your images unnecessarily in Photoshop

Below is a handy guide to help you calibrate your monitor so that it reproduces colours accurately.

Mac v PC
Mac monitors tend to have a brighter gamma setting than PC monitors, and this can make images that you've edited on a Mac look too dark when viewed on a PC. Prints from a Mac can also come out darker than you'd expect. If you're editing files to be viewed on a PC you can choose a PC Standard gamma setting when calibrating your display – this will help you create images that will look right on most PCs,

---

CLEVER CALIBRATION

Make sure your monitor is showing accurate contrast and colour

If you're using a PC you can tweak your display's contrast and colour settings by clicking the Adobe Gamma icon in the Control Panel. The Adobe Gamma Wizard will take you step-by-step through the process of adjusting your monitor's brightness, contrast and colour temperature settings. Mac users can tweak their monitor's gamma settings by going to the Displays section of the Systems Preferences menu. Click the Color tab, then press the Calibrate button. This will open the Display Calibrator Assistant, which, like the Adobe Gamma Wizard, takes you through a step-by-step monitor adjustment process.

Both Macs and PCs have built-in calibration tools that will help you to configure your display accurately

The Photoshop interface

Photoshop's default layout can be customised to suit the way you work, and the jobs you do

Default layout
If you've been tinkering with your workspace layout, and want to start from scratch with the default layout, go to Window > Workspace > Default Workspace – this should leave you with an interface very similar to the one shown in the annotated screenshot below. We're using Photoshop CS2 throughout this guide, but you'll find that the basic features highlighted are common to all recent versions of the program.

Once you've managed to configure your physical workspace by rearranging the furniture or sorting out the lighting, it's time to turn your attention to your virtual work area: the Photoshop interface. The program is highly customisable, and over the next few pages we'll show you how you can change the layout, by rearranging palettes and editing menus so that you can access the right tools for any job quickly and easily, and work more efficiently.

Photoshop is a huge package, and you can spend an awful lot of time wading through its various menus and sub-menus trying to find a particular tool or feature that you want to use. If you invest a little time setting up a personalised workspace you'll be able to radically streamline your image-editing workflow by making sure that the tools you use most often are always close to hand. We'll kick off by looking at the default Photoshop interface so that you'll know what we're referring to when we talk about features such as the options bar or the palette well.

THE DEFAULT WORKSPACE

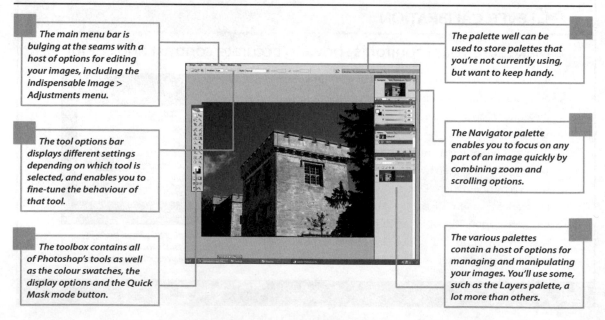

The main menu bar is bulging at the seams with a host of options for editing your images, including the indispensable Image > Adjustments menu.

The tool options bar displays different settings depending on which tool is selected, and enables you to fine-tune the behaviour of that tool.

The toolbox contains all of Photoshop's tools as well as the colour swatches, the display options and the Quick Mask mode button.

The palette well can be used to store palettes that you're not currently using, but want to keep handy.

The Navigator palette enables you to focus on any part of an image quickly by combining zoom and scrolling options.

The various palettes contain a host of options for managing and manipulating your images. You'll use some, such as the Layers palette, a lot more than others.

Customising the interface

You can streamline your image-editing workflow by rearranging and hiding palettes

Everyone knows that having a cluttered desk makes it hard to work efficiently. Discarded coffee cups and piles of paper can get in the way and slow you down as they compete for desk space with your mouse, monitor and keyboard. Even useful bits of kit such as Compact Flash card readers can take up valuable space, especially if they're not in constant use. By clearing your desk of such clutter you'll be better able to focus on the task of editing your images on your PC or Mac, and the same principle applies to your virtual workspace. Photoshop contains more than a dozen palettes, but you'll only use a few of them on a regular basis; the rest can be stored in the palette well, or closed down altogether if you know that you're not going to need them. You'll end up with a far leaner interface that will enable you to see more of your all-important images, and you'll be able to see the palettes you do need more easily. See below for our guide to the relative usefulness of a few of the palettes, and advice on how to manage them.

Saving your workspace
Once you've created your optimum image-editing layout you can save it by going to Window > Workspace > Save Workspace and labelling it appropriately – Photo Fixing, for example. You can store palette locations, and even keyboard shortcuts, in your saved workspace. If you subsequently move things around you can get your custom workspace back at any time by selecting it from the Workspace menu.

A MORE STREAMLINED WORKSPACE

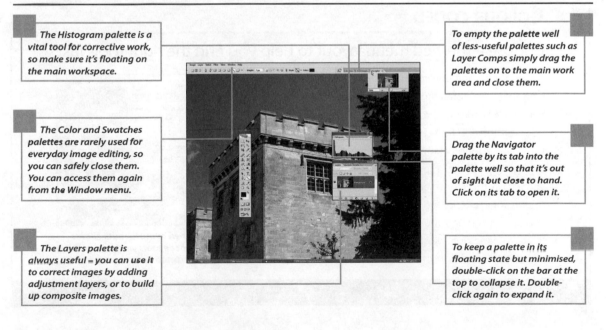

The Histogram palette is a vital tool for corrective work, so make sure it's floating on the main workspace.

The Color and Swatches palettes are rarely used for everyday image editing, so you can safely close them. You can access them again from the Window menu.

The Layers palette is always useful – you can use it to correct images by adding adjustment layers, or to build up composite images.

To empty the palette well of less-useful palettes such as Layer Comps simply drag the palettes on to the main work area and close them.

Drag the Navigator palette by its tab into the palette well so that it's out of sight but close to hand. Click on its tab to open it.

To keep a palette in its floating state but minimised, double-click on the bar at the top to collapse it. Double-click again to expand it.

Customising the menus

If you have CS2 you can configure the menus to make it easier to find the options you want

Relevant menus
Another workspace preset (see below) that's useful when you're correcting images is Image Analysis; the appropriate items (such as Image > Adjustments > Levels) are highlighted in green. Choosing a colour-coded workspace won't affect your custom palette layouts, so feel free to experiment with different workspace presets. The 'What's New in CS2' theme is handy if you've just bought the package.

Many of the tools that you'll use to work on your images are available in the floating palettes or the toolbox, and still more options can be found in the drop-down menus at the top of the Photoshop interface. In addition to photo retouching tools the menu also contains many commands that deal with topics such as typography, web optimisation and so on; many of these commands aren't relevant to the task of editing images, and wading through them to find the options you need can take time.

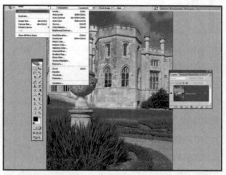

Photoshop's menus and sub-menus are packed with entries, making it difficult to find the more commonly used commands quickly

Fortunately CS2 offers several ways to help you find the menu options you're looking for more quickly.

COLOUR CODED

Choose a themed menu layout to help you find the right tools fast

To find the right menu commands for a particular job without being distracted by irrelevant options go to Window > Workspace. You'll see a list of themes, ranging from Automation to Web Design, and if you select one of these all the menu commands relevant to that theme will be highlighted with a specific colour, making it easier for you to pick them out. Select the Color and Tonal Correction option, for example, and click Yes in the dialog box that appears. Now when you open the menus you'll find that all the commands for adjusting the colours and tonal range of an image will be highlighted in orange.

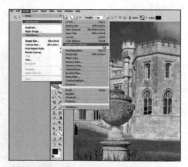

CS2's themed menu layouts enable you to find the tools you need without being distracted by irrelevant ones

Leaner and meaner

For the ultimate in customisation CS2 enables you to ditch unwanted menu items altogether

You've discovered how to create and save a customised workspace so that your favourite tools and palettes are visible, and how to use CS2's colour-coded menus to help you find the options you want fast. You can go one step further in your quest for a perfect workspace by removing unwanted options from CS2's menus altogether, enabling you to create an interface that's custom-built for image editing. Commands such as those relating to web images and animation, and even unwanted filters, can be

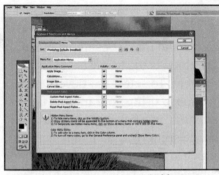

Some menu items won't be needed for image editing, so banish them from your workspace to streamline your workflow

banished from the menus, leaving you with a hand-picked selection of easy-to-find options.

Custom colouring
On the facing page we showed you how you can select colour-coded menu themes, and you can also colour-code menu items yourself to make it easier to find them. Go to Window > Workspace > Keyboard Shortcuts & Menus, and you'll see a Color column by each menu item. By default the colour is set to None, but you can call up a dialog that enables you to assign a colour to any item.

REMOVING MENU ITEMS

You can use CS2's Menus editor to hide unwanted commands

To remove menu items from your workspace go to Window > Workspace > Keyboard Shortcuts & Menus. Click the Menus tab, and make sure that Application Menus is selected. You can now click on the arrow button next to each menu heading, and scroll through a list of sub-menus. To hide unwanted items click on the Visibility button (the eye icon). For example, this guide is not concerned with editing images for use in various video formats, so you can hide the Pixel Aspect Ratio menu and all its sub-menus. You can hide individual sub-menu options, or click the parent menu to remove all sub-menu options in one go.

You can restore hidden commands to any menu by selecting Show All Menu Items from the foot of the menu

Keyboard shortcuts

Call up tools and commands by pressing a couple of keys, and create your own shortcuts

Identifying shortcuts
It's easy to see which menu items have a pre-assigned keyboard shortcut. Wade through the menus and sub-menus and you'll see that the shortcuts appear to the right of commands.

The right keys
To create a shortcut you must include the [Ctrl]/[Command] key and/or one of the function keys . You can also add the [Shift] key to the mix to give you more options. Don't be afraid to experiment, and feel free to override shortcuts that are assigned to tools you don't use. You can always undo changes you've made by going to Window > Workspace > Reset Keyboard Shortcuts in CS2, or by going to Edit > Keyboard Shortcuts in other versions and selecting Photoshop Defaults from the Set menu.

Another weapon in the fight against distracting interface clutter and time-consuming menu searching is the trusty keyboard shortcut. To select the Levels command using your mouse, for example, you have to go to the Image section of the main menu, and then open the Adjustments sub-menu – a faster way is to press [Ctrl]/[Command]+L. You'll find that some menu options, such as Photo Filter, don't have a default shortcut, and you can add a shortcut to any command by going to Window > Workspace > Keyboard Shortcuts & Menus in Photoshop CS2, or Edit > Keyboard Shortcuts in earlier versions. You'll find a list of menu sets, each containing the related sub-menus and their shortcuts; to add a new shortcut click in the Shortcut column for the appropriate menu item and type your desired key combination. If the shortcut you choose clashes with an existing shortcut Photoshop will display a warning – you can override the warning, or undo the change and enter an alternative shortcut.

SOME USEFUL SHORTCUTS

☐ **BY DEFAULT** the function keys (F1, F2 and so on) are assigned to particularly useful tools or commands. F1, for example, opens Photoshop's Help menu, while F12 applies the Revert command, which returns your image to the state it was in when you opened it. Mac users will find that their operating system has hijacked Photoshop's function keys for system tasks: F12 will fill the screen with widgets, for example! You can override this by going to Dashboard & Exposé in the Personal section of System Preferences.

☐ **F7** SHOWS OR HIDES the Layers palette. If you're working on a file with lots of layers your Layers palette will take up a lot of room, so you can close the other palettes, and hit F7 to call up the Layers palette as and when you need it.

☐ **TO** HIDE OR REVEAL all the palettes in your workspace hit the [Tab] key. To hide all the palettes except for the toolbox press [Shift]+[Tab].

Preferences

You can customise the way in which tools and features behave by editing the Preferences

1 Go to Edit > Preferences > General on a PC, or Photoshop > Preferences > General on a Mac. To start with make sure that Show Tool Tips is ticked in the Options section: when this is enabled a yellow text box will pop up when you hover your cursor over any tool in the toolbox, or over various settings in the options bar and palettes, giving a description of that tool or setting.

2 Most toolbox compartments contain more than one tool, and they all share the same keyboard shortcut (for example L for the Lasso tools). By default on a Mac you have to press [Shift]+L to toggle between the tools, but in General Preferences you can disable the Use Shift Key for Tool Switch option. You can then switch between tools by simply pressing the relevant key.

3 When you're editing an image you'll need to zoom in and out to see how your work is progressing. To use the Zoom Tool you have to swap it for the editing tool you're using, zoom in or out and then select your editing tool again. In CS2 and Elements 4 you can click the Zoom with Scroll Wheel option, which enables you to zoom without deselecting your editing tool.

4 By default the font size used for most of Photoshop's menus and palette labels is pretty small, and if you have CS2 you can increase the size – select Medium from the UI Font Size menu. You'll need to quit and restart Photoshop for this change to take effect – all other changes you make to the General Preferences will be implemented when you click OK in the dialog.

Tool information
If you have CS2 you can see more information about your currently selected tool in the Info palette. At the foot of the palette you'll see a couple of lines of text that tell you what the tool does.

Resetting Preferences
If you're not happy with your new Preferences settings, or simply want to start from scratch using Photoshop's default settings, quit Photoshop, and hold down [Ctrl]+[Alt]+[Shift] ([Command]+[Option]+ [Shift] on a Mac) when you relaunch it to restore the default settings.

Optimising your cursors

Use your tools more effectively by modifying their cursors to achieve pinpoint accuracy

Other cursors

In our annotated screenshot we suggest that you leave the Other Cursors option set to Standard. This is because it can be helpful to be able to identify the currently selected tool from its icon. If you want to temporarily turn a standard tool icon into a crosshair for more accurate editing, press the caps lock key.

On the previous page you learned how to modify the General Preferences to fine-tune the way the Photoshop interface looks and behaves, and to make your tool handling more effective you can choose from a selection of cursor styles. Go to the Display & Cursors section of the Preferences menu: you can do this using the drop-down menu in the Preferences dialog, or click the Next button twice to get there from the General Preferences page. As the default settings on a Mac and a PC are different, we'll

By default the Show Crosshair in Brush Tip option is enabled for the PC version of CS2, but not for the Mac version

explain the optimum settings that will enable you to use your brush-based tools with greater accuracy.

THE CURSOR OPTIONS

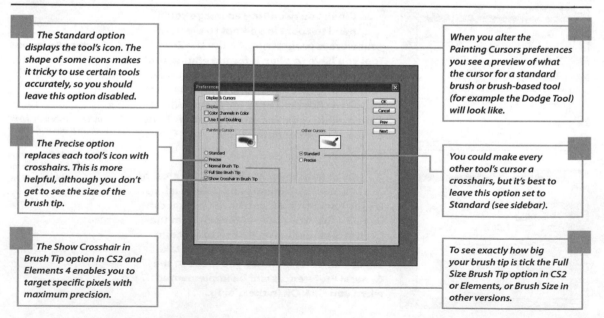

The Standard option displays the tool's icon. The shape of some icons makes it tricky to use certain tools accurately, so you should leave this option disabled.

The Precise option replaces each tool's icon with crosshairs. This is more helpful, although you don't get to see the size of the brush tip.

The Show Crosshair in Brush Tip option in CS2 and Elements 4 enables you to target specific pixels with maximum precision.

When you alter the Painting Cursors preferences you see a preview of what the cursor for a standard brush or brush-based tool (for example the Dodge Tool) will look like.

You could make every other tool's cursor a crosshairs, but it's best to leave this option set to Standard (see sidebar).

To see exactly how big your brush tip is tick the Full Size Brush Tip option in CS2 or Elements, or Brush Size in other versions.

Customising Elements

Elements users have a head start in terms of creating a dedicated photo-editing interface

Throughout this introductory chapter we've shown users of Photoshop CS2 (and earlier versions of the software) how they can trim their menus and customise their workspace to create an interface that's optimised for editing and retouching photos by hiding tools and commands that are rarely or never used. Users of Photoshop Elements will be pleased to find that they have a head start when it comes to customisation, as the program has been targeted firmly at the non-professional photography market. As a result, its interface is packed with tools that are dedicated to photo editing, and there's even a Quick Fix mode that's designed to enable you to correct common problems with the minimum of effort. Elements 4 even contains a new generation of photo fixing and selection tools that isn't available in CS2, so keep your eyes peeled for pages dedicated to these new tools – you may find that it's worth forking out £60 or so for the 'budget' version of Photoshop, even if you already own the full version.

The toolbox
The Elements toolbox initially appears to be docked to the left of the interface. To make it 'float' on the screen like Photoshop's toolbox click in the top panel above the Move and Zoom tools, and drag the toolbox on to the main work area.

CUSTOMISING ELEMENTS' STANDARD EDIT INTERFACE

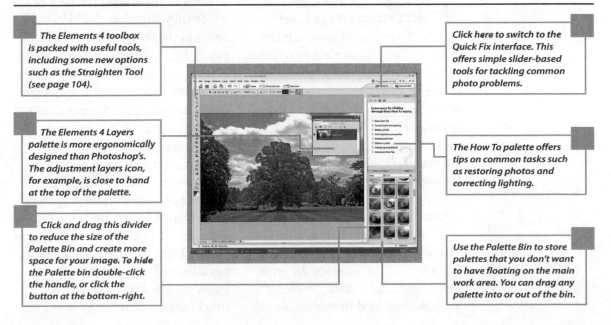

The Elements 4 toolbox is packed with useful tools, including some new options such as the Straighten Tool (see page 104).

The Elements 4 Layers palette is more ergonomically designed than Photoshop's. The adjustment layers icon, for example, is close to hand at the top of the palette.

Click and drag this divider to reduce the size of the Palette Bin and create more space for your image. To hide the Palette bin double-click the handle, or click the button at the bottom-right.

Click here to switch to the Quick Fix interface. This offers simple slider-based tools for tackling common photo problems.

The How To palette offers tips on common tasks such as restoring photos and correcting lighting.

Use the Palette Bin to store palettes that you don't want to have floating on the main work area. You can drag any palette into or out of the bin.

Chapter 2

CORRECTING AND ENHANCING YOUR COLOURS

Photoshop boasts a variety of tools that will enable you to restore an image's true colours quickly and effectively, and in this chapter we'll show you how to get the best out of them

The human eye is a sophisticated bit of kit, and it can generally discern the colour of objects under different lighting conditions without too much trouble. But while we take colour perception for granted, it's worth learning a little of the theory because it has a bearing on how cameras capture colour, and how this information is handled by Photoshop. By understanding how colour is perceived you'll be better able to fix colour-related problems.

The science bit

Light is made up of many different wavelengths, and these wavelengths are perceived as different colours by our brains, depending on the way in which they stimulate the rods and cones in the retina at the back of the eye. When light hits an object some of the wavelengths are absorbed, and so are invisible to the eye, while others are reflected, and are detected by the eye. It's this process that determines an object's colour.

The human eye is not perfect, however, and it can struggle to perceive colours in certain lighting conditions. The sun emits the full spectrum of light wavelengths, but if the light source falling on an object has a limited range of wavelengths (such as light from certain types of street lamps), then it may not contain

Page 25 *Know your enemy – learn to spot common colour-related problems*

Page 27 *Use adjustment layers to edit images without destroying information*

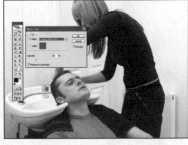

Page 28 *Use the preset Photo Filter options to banish colour casts in seconds*

Page 31 *Find out how to correct colour using Photoshop's Camera Raw editor*

Page 33 *Remove red-eye from a group of people with one click in Elements*

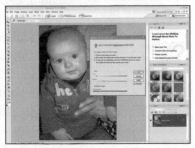

Page 35 *Use Elements' unique colour correction tools to improve skin tones*

any colours that can be reflected by the objects it's illuminating, and this is why it's impossible for us to see an object's true colours with the naked eye in certain conditions.

The digital 'eye'

A digital camera is modelled closely on the human eye. Reflected light enters the lens (the 'cornea'), passes through the aperture (the 'iris') and hits a sensor (the 'retina') which decodes and processes the colour information. However, just like our eyes the camera can struggle to perceive colour correctly, and it's also a much less sophisticated tool: this can lead to all kinds of colour-related problems with our photos, particularly those that are captured in less-than-ideal lighting conditions.

In this chapter we'll show you how to identify these problems, and how to deal with them. You'll discover how the colour temperature of different light can add casts to your images, and how you can use various tools and techniques to remove them. We'll also show you how to remove red-eye with the minimum of fuss, and a host of other colour correction tips and tricks. You might feel a little overwhelmed by the sheer variety of options Photoshop gives you for editing colours, but we'll help you to choose the right tool for every job.

Colour temperature

Understand what causes colour casts so you can produce correctly white-balanced shots

Changing settings
When you use white balance presets like Daylight or Tungsten you can get more faithful colours than if you leave the setting at Auto. However, it's easy to forget to change the setting when you move from one location to another. If you use an indoor Tungsten setting outdoors you'll be cooling down an already cool scene, and your shot will take on a blue cast.

Photographs are often marred by a cast or tint that discolours the image – usually this tint is either a 'cool' blue or a 'warm' orange. By understanding what causes colour casts you'll be able to deal with them more effectively, or even avoid the problem altogether by choosing the appropriate white balance setting on your camera.

The problem of colour casts exists because different light sources have different colour temperatures. To put it simply, daylight is blue and indoor light is orange. The human eye is able to perceive colours accurately both indoors and out, but a digital camera needs to perform an adjustment in order to capture colours correctly. The camera will try to warm up or cool down a shot, so that any white objects in the scene appear white, rather than blue or orange – this is why the camera's white balance feature is so named. When you take a photo you can give the camera information about the prevailing colour temperature by selecting the correct white balance setting – see below for a guide.

The Kelvin scale
The colour temperature of light is measured in degrees Kelvin (after Lord Kelvin, the 19th century scientist who identified the phenomenon). The temperature of natural light varies depending on the time of day and lighting conditions, while that of artificial light depends on the light source. In general, daylight has a colour temperature of around 5,200K, and indoor tungsten light is around 3,200K.

CAMERA WHITE BALANCE SETTINGS

☐ **AUTO** – On this setting the camera attempts to deal with light with a colour temperature varying from 3,000 – 7,000K. The camera can easily be confused, so it's a better idea to select one of the following presets.

☐ **DAYLIGHT** – If you tell the camera that it's shooting outdoors it'll know that daylight is cool (5,200K), and will warm up the shot to compensate.

☐ **CLOUDY** – If the sun pops behind a cloud the light's colour temperature will fall to a cooler 6,000K, and this setting warms the shot further.

☐ **TUNGSTEN** – Indoor light has a warmer colour temperature of around 3,200K, and this setting will cause the camera to cool down the shot to remove the orange tint.

☐ **FLASH** – This setting will enable you to capture accurate colours when you're using flash indoors. A burst of flash has a colour temperature similar to that of a cloudy day.

Common colour casts

Your camera's white balance settings can create tints that will ruin your shots unless corrected

1 Although this image was taken in daylight the camera was left on an indoor Tungsten setting, so the camera has cooled down the image in an attempt to capture tint-free colours: this makes the blue daylight look even bluer. Mixed light conditions can also confuse the camera, even when the white balance is set to Auto (see sidebar).

2 Another common colour tint caused by an incorrect white balance setting is a warm orange, which occurs when the camera warms up light that already has a warm colour temperature. This can happen if you're shooting indoors and forget to change the camera's Daylight setting to Tungsten, and will result in orange-tinted shots like this one.

3 The light from an electronic flash has a similar colour temperature to that of a cloudy day (around 6,000K), so when you're shooting indoors you shouldn't necessarily use an indoor white balance setting if you're using flash, as this can lead to cold-looking shots with bleached-out skin tones. Some digital cameras offer a special white balance setting just for flashguns.

4 Although you can use several Photoshop tools to remove colour casts there's a danger of adding unwanted noise and artifacts to your pictures during the editing process. There's no substitute for shooting the image correctly in the first place, as we can see from this correctly balanced shot that contains white whites instead of blue or orange tints.

Fluorescent
Many high-end digital SLRs have additional white balance settings for dealing with a range of other colour temperature scenarios, such as shooting under fluorescent light. Fluorescent light has a cooler colour temperature (around 3,800K) than tungsten light, and tends to add a green tint to shots: the Fluorescent setting counteracts this.

Mixed light
Scenes that have a mix of bright light and dull shade can confuse the camera's Auto white balance setting. The camera might attempt to balance the colours for the areas in direct sunlight by cooling them down; however, the cooler shaded areas would also be cooled down, making them appear too cold (blue). This will result in a shot with correctly balanced colours in the sunlit areas, but cool colour casts in the shadows.

The Color Balance command

The Color Balance dialog enables you to correct colour casts, but it's not a 'quick fix' option

Colour theory
When you're using the Color Balance dialog it helps if you have some knowledge of colour theory, and particularly the colour wheel, which represents the colours of the visible spectrum in circular form. For example, blue and yellow are on the opposite sides of the colour wheel, so to remove a blue cast from an image you need to drag the yellow/blue slider towards yellow.

When we view an object with the naked eye the cones in our retinas interpret reds, greens and blues to reproduce that object's colour, and in the standard RGB editing mode Photoshop reproduces colours by mixing red, green and blue colour channels. The Color Balance dialog (Image > Adjustments > Color Balance) enables you to remix Photoshop's RGB channels by dragging sliders to correct colour casts, and you can also make targeted corrections to a image's shadows, midtones and highlights. This all sounds useful in theory, although in practice it can take you a rather long time to fix a photo if you're adjusting all three tonal areas. So, while you can get some very good results with the Color Balance dialog, for faster colour cast removal it makes sense to use a tool that's dedicated to that specific purpose, such as the Photo Filter command (see page 28). Note that the Color Balance command isn't available in Elements, as the program doesn't support channels, but Photo Filter is included.

THE COLOR BALANCE DIALOG

These channel readouts show the percentage of red green and blue that you're adding or subtracting from your image.

Access the Color Balance menu by going to Image > Adjustments > Color Balance.

Tick Preserve Luminosity to maintain the image's tonal balance, and prevent brightness values being affected by your changes.

To see how your image looks with and without the adjustment applied, toggle the Preview option.

The Tone Balance section enables you to target your colour correction at the image's shadows, midtones or highlights.

To warm up a cool shot you need to reduce the amount of blue: you can do this by dragging the yellow/blue slider towards yellow.

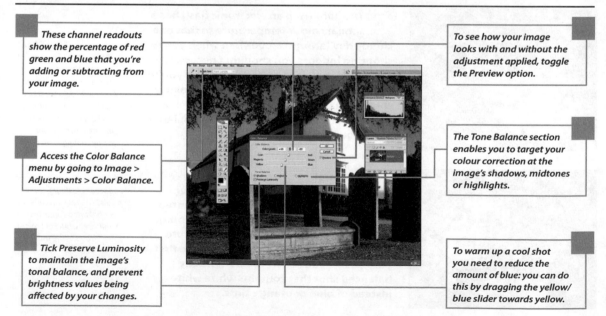

Fine-tuning corrections

Fine-tune your colour edits using the Fade command, or better still use adjustment layers

After you've applied an adjustment such as Color Balance to an image you can fine-tune the effect by selecting the Fade option from the Edit menu: a dialog box will pop up in which you can drag a slider to reduce the strength of the adjustment. However, it's important to remember that when you make major alterations directly to a photo's colours or tones, you're permanently changing that image's pixels once you click the OK button. For this reason it's generally best to perform your editing either on a

You can reduce the intensity of your Color Balance adjustment immediately after applying it by going to Edit > Fade

duplicate layer (see sidebar) or an adjustment layer – see below for more on this latter option.

Duplicating layers
To duplicate a layer drag its thumbnail on to the 'Create a new layer' button in the Layers palette. You can then edit this copy layer secure in the knowledge that your original image information won't be changed. Note that this will increase the size of your file, while adding an adjustment layer will have little or no effect on file size. However, some edits can't be applied on adjustment layers, so you'll have no option but to make a copy.

ADJUSTMENT LAYERS

Adjustment layers enable you to work with maximum flexibility

As we mentioned above, if you apply edits direct to an image layer information on that layer will be altered permanently. Adjustment layers enable you to edit without affecting the original image information, and this gives you the freedom to experiment wIthout fear of ruining your photo. Adjustment layers are overlaid on the layer you're editing; you can turn them on and off by clicking the eye icon to the left of the layer thumbnail to see how they affect an image, and reduce their opacity in the Layers palette to reduce the strength of the effect. They remain intact even after a file has been closed, so you can go back and tweak your edits at any time.

Adjustment layers enable you to fine-tune your colour corrections at any stage in the photo-fixing process

The Photo Filter dialog

Remove colour casts with a single click using this simple but highly effective option

Elements 4
If you want to use Photo Filter in Elements 4 you'll find that, while it's not available under the Enhance > Adjust Color menu, it is available as an adjustment layer. When you add the adjustment layer the dialog will open, and you can use the steps outlined below to cool down the orange tint in our source image, or to warm up a photo.

The Color Balance command has been available since the earliest versions of Photoshop, but it wasn't designed specifically to fix colour cast problems, and with more and more photographers using Photoshop, Adobe created a tool dedicated to removing colour casts more effectively. The Photo Filter dialog saves you the hassle of fiddling with sliders by providing you with a selection of preset adjustments that are designed to combat problems such as orange or blue tints. As well as removing casts,

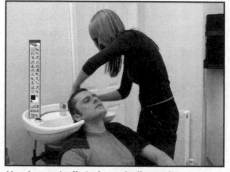

Here's a typically 'colour-challenged' image. A Photo Filter adjustment will instantly cool down the warm tint

Photo Filter also enables you get creative by tinting your shots, for example to add a sepia effect.

USING PHOTO FILTER

Open the dialog, select a filter – and your colour cast is history!

Open the file Tungsten.jpg from the CD. This warm shot needs to be cooled down, so go to Image > Adjustments > Photo Filter (or add a Photo Filter adjustment layer) and select Cooling Filter (80) from the menu. This immediately restores the walls in the shot to a tint-free white, while the skin tones also take on a more natural hue, which greatly improves the picture. If you have a cold-looking shot you can warm it up by selecting Warming Filter (85). You can increase or reduce the effect by adjusting the Density slider, and you can also change the filter colour, although for removing colour casts the default orange and blue are fine.

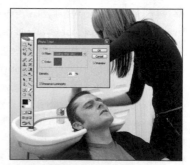

The Photo Filter command has removed the colour cast from this image very effectively

Setting the white point

For a more precise solution to colour casts you'll need to turn to the Levels command

Compared to the Color Balance command the Photo Filter provides a much quicker and easier way of warming up or cooling down images that have colour casts. Often the default Photo Filter presets will be enough to correctly warm or cool shots, but as some casts are stronger than others you might have to spend time experimenting with the Photo Filter's Density slider, or change the filter color. An alternative and potentially quicker approach to removing casts is to specify which colours in an image should be pure white, and have Photoshop apply a global correction based on this information. To do this go to Image > Adjustments > Levels, and select the Set White Point eyedropper from the bottom-right of the dialog. Click on a tinted part of the image that you know should be pure white (the white of an eye, for example): Photoshop will warm up or cool down the image accordingly to remove the colour cast. You could also use the Set Black Point or Set Gray Point eyedroppers, but it's easiest to spot casts in white areas.

RGB values
Pure white pixels have a value of 255 for each of the red, green and blue channels, while pure black pixels have RGB values of 0; all other colours are made up of different combinations of RGB values. When you're moving around an image with the eyedropper you can see the RGB value of the pixel beneath your cursor in the Info palette: this can help you to identify pixels that are almost white, but have a slight tint.

EYEDROPPERS IN ELEMENTS

Remove colour casts in a click using Photoshop Elements

The Levels eyedropper technique demonstrated above is so effective at correcting colour casts that in Elements 4 it has been rebranded as a dedicated colour cast removal tool, and given a starring role in the main menu. Go to Enhance > Adjust Color > Remove Color Cast. A dialog will appear instructing you to click on a tinted area that should be either pure black, grey or white. Zoom in if necessary so you can make out the colour of individual pixels, and click. Elements will analyse the colour of the sampled pixel to see if it has a blue or orange tint, and will then warm up or cool down the entire image accordingly to remove the colour cast.

Restore tinted images to their true colours with a quick click of the Remove Color Cast eyedropper

The Variations command

This dialog displays multiple previews of a shot to steer you through the correction process

Variations in Elements
A slightly less sophisticated version of the Variations dialog is available in Elements – go to Enhance > Adjust Color > Color Variations. In both versions, as well as enabling you to remove colour tints the dialog enables you to adjust the intensity of the image's overall colour intensity by clicking the Saturation button – this is particularly useful for shots that have been 'bleached' by flash.

All the tint-tackling tools we've examined so far have their particular strengths and weaknesses. The Color Balance command (page 26) can certainly remove a colour cast, but if you haven't got a good grasp of colour theory then you could be experimenting with sliders for a long time before you get a tint-free photo. The eyedropper-based techniques on the previous page can create a correctly balanced image in a single click, although if you don't click in the right place then you can get very strange results, and may add even more dramatic colour casts to your image. Photo Filter is the quickest and easiest option, although unlike Color Balance it doesn't enable you to target the shadow, midtone and highlight areas independently. There is, however, one other option that's well worth checking out – the Variations dialog. Variations has the same channel-mixing power that the Color Balance dialog offers, but comes with a more user-friendly interface that displays thumbnail previews to guide you through the correction process.

VARIATIONS IN ACTION

You can warm up a cool, flash-bleached shot in no time…

Open the file Flash.jpg from the CD. Due to a daylight white balance setting and a blast of flash this indoors shot is too cool, giving our young subject an unhealthy pale look. Instead of dragging sliders around and hoping for the best go to Image > Adjustments > Variations, and by comparing the previews you'll be able to see exactly how the image will look if you add or subtract a specific colour. Click the Highlights button, as the highlights are where the blue tint is most evident, and click the More Red thumbnail, as the preview indicates that this will bring a healthier tinge to the baby's cheeks, and banish the blue cast.

Click a thumbnail to adjust the image. You can target shadows, midtones, highlights or saturation values

Color balancing RAW files

If image quality is your priority shoot Raw files, and correct them with the Camera Raw plug-in

Photoshop offers different colour correction tools for people with different levels of expertise, and if you don't want to know about colour temperature and RGB channels then Photo Filter is your best bet. At the other extreme, if you want to edit the white balance setting at which a shot was taken you can do so, as long as your camera can shoot Raw files and your version of Photoshop features the Camera Raw plug-in. Open the file CRW_1460.CRW. This image was taken with the white balance set to 4,300K, which is designed to cool

Setting White Balance to As Shot in the Adjust tab shows us that this daylight shot was taken using an indoor colour temperature setting

down tungsten light. As the subject is in cool daylight the image has a blue tint, particularly in the shadows.

Raw.mov
In the video tutorial on the CD we'll talk you through using the Adobe Camera Raw editor to correct your image's colour balance. You'll see how easy it is to use the one-click White Balance Tool to remove colour casts, and discover how to use the White Balance menu presets to correct images taken in almost any lighting conditions. The movie also covers correcting Raw images in Elements 4.

CORRECTING COLOUR IN CAMERA RAW

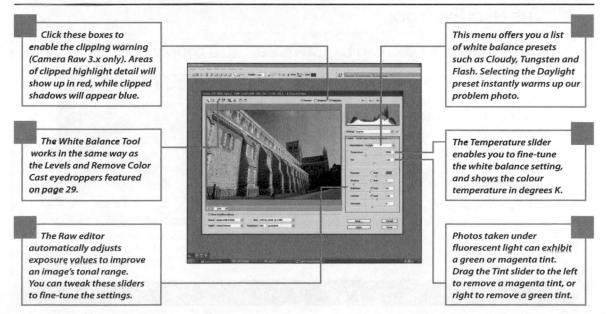

Click these boxes to enable the clipping warning (Camera Raw 3.x only). Areas of clipped highlight detail will show up in red, while clipped shadows will appear blue.

The White Balance Tool works in the same way as the Levels and Remove Color Cast eyedroppers featured on page 29.

The Raw editor automatically adjusts exposure values to improve an image's tonal range. You can tweak these sliders to fine-tune the settings.

This menu offers you a list of white balance presets such as Cloudy, Tungsten and Flash. Selecting the Daylight preset instantly warms up our problem photo.

The Temperature slider enables you to fine-tune the white balance setting, and shows the colour temperature in degrees K.

Photos taken under fluorescent light can exhibit a green or magenta tint. Drag the Tint slider to the left to remove a magenta tint, or right to remove a green tint.

Removing red-eye

Red-eye is the bane of many a flash photo – here's how to get rid of it using Photoshop

Red Eye.mov
Check out the video tutorial on the CD to see red-eye eradicated quickly and effectively. We'll show you how to remove red-eye in CS2, pre-CS2 versions of Photoshop and Elements 4 using the techniques demonstrated on these pages, and throw in a few extra tips as well.

Red-eye spoils many a portrait photo, and is caused by camera flash reflecting off the blood vessels at the back of a subject's eyes, causing their pupils to turn red. To fix the problem in pre-CS2 versions of Photoshop first select the pupils with the Elliptical Marquee Tool (M). Go to Image > Adjustments > Hue/Saturation, select Reds from the Edit menu and drag the Saturation slider to the left to remove all traces of red (you may need to target Magentas as well); to darken the pupil drag the Lightness

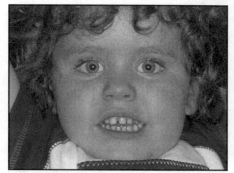

Red-eye can turn a cute child into a little monster! Fortunately you can remove it using a variety of tools in Photoshop and Elements

slider left. If you've got CS2 you can use the dedicated Red Eye Tool to fix the problem in seconds.

THE RED EYE TOOL

If you've got CS2 you can banish red-eye in a couple of clicks

To put CS2's Red Eye Tool through its paces (or to practice any of the techniques featured on these two pages) open RedEye.jpg from the CD and select the tool – it shares a toolbox compartment with the Spot Healing Brush (press [Shift]+[Control]+J to cycle through the tools in that compartment). It usually works 'out of the box', although you can tweak the default Pupil Size and Darken Amount settings in the options bar if necessary. All you need to do is click on each red pupil and it'll turn black, and the tool is intelligent enough to correct red pixels in the eyes without altering similarly coloured pixels in the rest of the image.

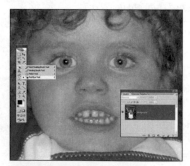

CS2's Red Eye Tool enables you to restore your subjects' pupils to a healthy black in seconds

Red-eye removal in Elements 4

Elements has its own version of the Red Eye Tool, and also has another trick up its sleeve

Photoshop Elements is optimised for the quick and easy fixing of digital photos, and not surprisingly red-eye removal is a key feature. The Red Eye Removal Tool (Y) in Elements 3 and 4 is housed in its own toolbox compartment to indicate its importance, and although the name is slightly different it works in exactly the same way as CS2's Red Eye Tool – you simply have to click on a pupil to turn in black, and you can also change the Pupil Size and Darken Amount settings in the options bar. While you might think

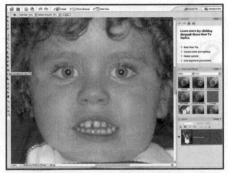

The Red Eye Removal Tool in Elements 3 and 4 eliminates red-eye just as thoroughly, and just as quickly, as CS2's Red Eye Tool

that fixing red-eye couldn't get any easier than this, you'd be wrong! See below for an even faster solution…

Auto Red Eye Fix
You don't even need to have the Red Eye Removal Tool selected to remove red-eye in Elements! Open an image, go to the main menu and select Enhance > Auto Red Eye Fix ([Ctrl]/[Command]+R) to remove all examples of red-eye from the shot. You'll also find the Red Eye Removal Tool in Elements' Quick Fix editing interface, as well as an Auto Red Eye Fix option in the General Fixes section.

AUTO RED-EYE REMOVAL

Remove every instance of red-eye from a shot with a single click!

You may find it hard to believe that there's an even quicker way to eradicate red-eye in Elements 4 – after all, what could be faster than clicking once in each eye? – but because Elements 4 is designed specifically for fixing digital photos it boasts some unique tools. Open a photo containing several subjects with red-eye, select the Red Eye Removal Tool, and take a look at the options bar. Unlike CS2's Red Eye Tool, the options bar features an extra button marked Auto. When you click this Elements scans the entire image, and removes every instance of red-eye in one fell swoop. It's great for group shots, as you don't have to click on each pupil in turn.

Elements 4 enables you to eradicate multiple instances of red-eye from a group shot in a single click

Quick Fix in Elements 4

Correct colour-related problems in a jiffy using the appropriately named Quick Fix interface

Pick and mix
Some of the Standard Edit tools are available to you when you're in Quick Fix mode, so you can combine the Quick Fix colour tools with colour correcting tools from the main menu bar. You could, for example, select the Remove Color Cast option from the main menu, and then fine-tune your image's colours using the Temperature and Tint sliders in the Color section of the Quick Fix interface.

On the previous page we pointed you in the direction of Elements 4's Quick Fix interface, and its Auto Red Eye Fix button. Elements' Standard Edit interface is a cut-down version of Photoshop, featuring the tools most useful to digital photographer; click on the Quick Fix button and you get an even more streamlined interface, with the most useful image-editing tools under one roof. This saves you having to rummage around in the main menu, as most of the tools you need, including variants of the

The Quick Fix interface gives you access to the most useful image-editing tools, enabling you to correct common photo problems fast

colour-correction tools we've looked at in this chapter, are displayed in a mini toolbox and themed palettes.

Before and after
When you're editing an image's colours in Quick Fix mode it makes sense to see how your edited version compares to the original. If you go to the View menu at the bottom-left of the interface and choose Before and After, any changes you make to the image's colours will appear in the After image on the right. If you're unhappy with your editing, start again by clicking the Reset button above the After version of the image.

COLOUR CORRECTION IN QUICK FIX

☐ **THE COLOR PALETTE** has all the tools you need to combat typical colour problems, such as a warm orange tint. The Auto button is always worth a click, as it's designed to improve both colour and contrast.

☐ **DRAGGING THE HUE** slider will change the colours in an image dramatically. It's not particularly useful for correction work, but it can be used creatively.

☐ **THE TEMPERATURE SLIDER** makes correcting white balance problems easy. Drag the slider to the left to cool down warm shots, or drag it to the right to warm up cool shots.

☐ **AFTER YOU'VE COOLED DOWN** your colours using the Temperature slider you may find that there's a greenish tint to the whites in the shot. Drag the Tint slider to the right to remove this tint, so that whites appear white and skin tones look natural.

Correcting skin tones

You can restore colour to anyone's cheeks using a unique correction tool in Elements 4

On page 30 we used the Variations dialog to warm up a rather cold-looking baby portrait. The Variations command isn't specifically designed to sort out incorrect colour balance, although it does a decent enough job, and while Elements 4 users have access to their own version of the Variations command (Enhance > Adjust Color > Color Variations), a better option for fixing people shots is the Adjust Color for Skin Tone command. This tool is designed to restore colour to washed-out skin tones, and you can

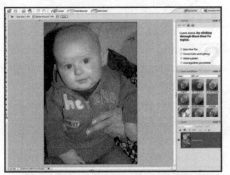

As we saw earlier, a close encounter with a flash has bleached this baby's skin tones and added a cold blue tint, but we can easily fix the image

tweak the image's colour temperature to fine-tune the correction – see below for a guide to using it.

Pros and cons
Although the Adjust Color for Skin Tone command is effective at enhancing washed-out or incorrectly white-balanced skin tones, it does have a downside. The tool adjusts all the colours in the image, not just skin tones, and this means that it could add a colour cast to other parts of the image, such as a person's clothes or surrounding scenery.

A HEALTHIER COMPLEXION

Click on an area of skin, then fine-tune things using the sliders

Open the file Flash.jpg from the CD in Elements 4. Go to the main menu and choose Enhance > Adjust Color > Adjust Color for Skin Tone. When the dialog opens move your cursor over the image, and it will change to an eyedropper. Click on a cool blue section of the subject's skin. Elements will analyse the sample, and attempt to warm up the photo to produce a correctly colour-balanced skin tone. We don't need to tan our toddler, so drag the Tan slider to the left, and drag the Blush slider right for a healthier complexion. You can also warm up the skin's colour temperature by dragging the Ambient Light slider to the right.

Correct cold-looking or colourless skin quickly with Elements 4's unique Adjust Color for Skin Tone command

From correction to creation

Move from colour correction to more creative editing using adjustment layers and brushes

Paint with Light.mov
To see our 'Painting with light' walkthrough demonstrated, and pick up some extra image-editing tips, check out the video tutorial on your CD.

On page 27 we introduced you to the concept of adjustment layers, and demonstrated how these powerful tools can be used to edit an image without permanently altering its pixels. You can add as many adjustment layers as you like to an image to perform a variety of colour or other corrections, and you can experiment by altering the opacity of layers, turn layers on and off to see how your editing is going, and localise your edits by painting on a layer's mask with brushes. In addition to using adjustment layers

This daylight shot can be dramatically enhanced to mimic a specialised photography effect using adjustment layers

to correct an image you can also use them more creatively, as you'll see on the facing page.

PAINTING WITH LIGHT

See how this effect is created before mimicking it in Photoshop

On the facing page we'll show you how to use adjustment layers to recreate the 'painting with light' photographic effect. This normally involves going to a location at night and placing your camera on a tripod. You then have to set your camera to take a very long exposure – this gives you time to run around with a hand-held flash and illuminate parts of a building or other scene, and the bursts of light create dramatic pools of light against contrasting shadows. As you can imagine, this technique is time-consuming, and very hard to get right, but thanks to the versatility of adjustment layers you can paint with light at your leisure.

Follow the walkthrough on the facing page to turn day to night and create dramatic pools of light

Painting with light

Use an adjustment layer to alter the colour of a photo, and then edit it to create 'pools' of light

1 Open the source file Painting.jpg. Click the 'Create new fill or adjustment layer' in the Layers palette and choose Levels from the menu. Dramatically darken the entire image by dragging the white Output Levels slider left until its reading is 130, and click OK. (Don't worry about how the Levels dialog works for now – we'll look at it more closely in the next chapter.)

The right image
If you want to apply the 'painting with light' effect to one of your own images choose a subject that was shot in direct sunlight, or on an overcast day. Don't use a shot that has starkly contrasting areas of light and shade, as this is the effect that you're going to create digitally.

2 Select the Brush Tool (B). Open the Brush Preset picker in the options bar, and scroll down to choose a soft-edged brush with a diameter of 300 pixels. Make sure the foreground colour is set to black in the toolbox – if it isn't, press D to restore the swatches to their default black foreground and white background colours.

3 Click the adjustment layer's mask icon in the thumbnail to target the mask (the right-hand icon; the left-hand icon is the adjustment icon), and start painting. As you apply the black brush to the mask you remove the darkening adjustment, and reveal the brighter original image on the Background layer; this creates the illusion of pools of light cutting through the darkness.

More about masks
On page 56 we'll show you how to use layer masks to make parts of a layer partially transparent so that you can blend two images together to solve exposure problems. We'll also be taking a closer look at using layer masks to modify selections on page 80.

4 Add as many pools of light as you like to create a suitably atmospheric scene. To make the image look more nocturnal you can cool down its colour temperature by adding a Hue/Saturation adjustment layer at the top of the stack, ticking the Colorize box, and dragging the Hue slider to around 210 to render the image in cool blue tones.

Infra-red film effect

Remove the colour from an image altogether to create the surreal look of infra-red photography

The real thing
Like the painting with light technique, infra-red photography is something that you can attempt on location. Shooting with an infra-red filter over the lens is tricky, however, because infra-red light has a longer wavelength than visible light, so you'll need a longer exposure, which means you'll need to use a tripod. It's also harder to focus using an IR filter, so all in all the Photoshop method is a great deal easier!

Most of this chapter has focused on techniques that enable you to correct colours, so that what you see through the viewfinder is accurately represented on screen and in print. Colours are created by visible light waves reflecting off the objects that they hit, but you can use Photoshop to go one step further and simulate light waves that are invisible to the human eye, such as light at the infra-red end of the spectrum. Infra-red (or IR light) can be photographed using special filters (see sidebar). This creates

To fake an infra-red shot convincingly choose an image with a clear sky and some vegetation, such as the tree in this image

striking monochrome images in which the sky turns dark, and green vegetation glows white.

CREATING AN INFRA-RED IMAGE

Remove the colour from the duplicated version of your shot by going to Image > Adjustments > Desaturate.

Go to image > Adjustments > Invert (or press [Control]+I to create a negative-style version of your monochrome image that closely mimics the effect of an infra-red filter.

Vegetation reflects infra-red light and so appears white. This helps to create striking inverted silhouettes against the black sky.

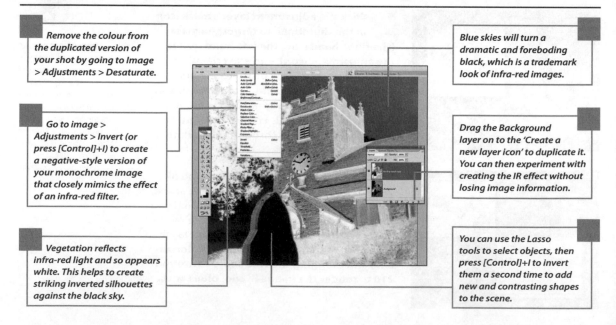

Blue skies will turn a dramatic and foreboding black, which is a trademark look of infra-red images.

Drag the Background layer on to the 'Create a new layer icon' to duplicate it. You can then experiment with creating the IR effect without losing image information.

You can use the Lasso tools to select objects, then press [Control]+I to invert them a second time to add new and contrasting shapes to the scene.

Cross-processing effect

Go wild with your colour editing to create an effect that has its origins in the darkroom

W e'll finish off our chapter on colour editing by showing you how to re-create a photographic technique that can give your image's colours a creative twist. When film photographers develop slide or print film they need to use the appropriate chemicals for that file, and if you develop print film using chemicals designed for slide film then you get some bizarre results. Colours become strikingly oversaturated and surreal, and the contrast becomes more striking too, giving the shot extra impact. Cross-processing can

The cross-processing look works particularly well with 'urban landscape' Images, lifting their familiar colours to a new, surreal level

also add grain to images, creating the kinds of textures that you might capture using a high ISO setting.

CrossProcess.jpg
You can use the file on the CD to follow the steps in the annotated screenshot below and create a cross-processed colour effect. This technique turns a mundane urban shot into something much more striking, with dreamlike colours and harsher contrast.

CREATING THE CROSS-PROCESSED LOOK

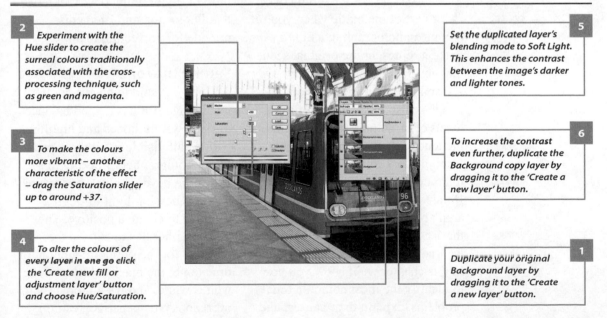

2 Experiment with the Hue slider to create the surreal colours traditionally associated with the cross-processing technique, such as green and magenta.

3 To make the colours more vibrant – another characteristic of the effect – drag the Saturation slider up to around +37.

4 To alter the colours of every layer in one go click the 'Create new fill or adjustment layer' button and choose Hue/Saturation.

5 Set the duplicated layer's blending mode to Soft Light. This enhances the contrast between the image's darker and lighter tones.

6 To increase the contrast even further, duplicate the Background copy layer by dragging it to the 'Create a new layer' button.

1 Duplicate your original Background layer by dragging it to the 'Create a new layer' button.

CORRECTING EXPOSURE PROBLEMS

Photoshop has a variety of tools to help you correct the tonal range of your images. We'll show you how to use them to produce images with strong contrast and maximum detail

Correcting colour is only one part of the battle when you're editing a photograph in a bid to make it represent the original scene that you captured more accurately. As well as colour information, an image is also made up of differing levels of brightness that determine the tone of these colours, ranging from the darkest shadows, via the midtones to the brightest highlights. If the tones of a scene or subject aren't properly defined then a shot that's correctly colour-balanced and well-composed can easily be ruined. In this chapter we'll show you how to identify the most common tonal problems, explain their causes, and

introduce you to the powerful tools that Photoshop and Elements provide for correcting them.

Setting the tone

An image is said to have a good tonal range if it has a good balance of shadows, midtones and highlights, with detail visible in all three areas. Film photographers working in a darkroom develop black-and-white shots by passing light through a negative to create a positive. The photographer has to expose the negative for the optimum amount of time to get the blacks black and the whites white, and it's all too easy to overexpose the negative, resulting in

Page 43 Use the Histogram palette to diagnose common exposure problems

Page 44 The Levels dialog enables you to lighten underexposed photos fast

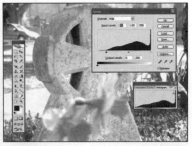

Page 45 Overexposed shots can also be corrected using the Levels sliders

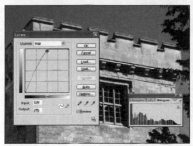

Page 48 Use the powerful Curves dialog for precise tonal adjustments

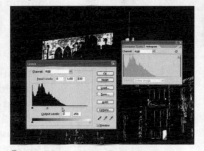

Page 50 Use a visual guide to help you avoid clipping highlights or shadows

Page 57 Combine two exposures to create one perfectly-balanced shot

an image containing washed-out blacks that look grey, and blown highlights with little or no detail. Alternatively, the photographer might underexpose the image, and end up with a print featuring overly-dark shadows and dull highlights.

Causes and cures

Digital photographers face similar challenges when it comes to creating an image with a healthy tonal range. We don't use negatives and don't have to develop our own film, but we can still encounter problems due to incorrect exposure settings on our cameras. We can easily end up with shots that have no detail in the shadows or highlights, as well as shots that look drab and washed-out. Shooting high-contrast scenes with bright skies and dark foregrounds can also cause problems; set to Auto the camera can become confused and expose to capture detail in the sky, turning the foreground into a silhouette devoid of detail.

Fortunately Photoshop has a huge range of tools and commands for correcting an image's exposure, as well as tools to help you diagnose problems accurately. We'll show you how to choose the right solution for any challenge, so that you can produce images with a perfect tonal range every time.

Common exposure problems

Learn to recognise the causes of typical tonal problems so that you can fix them effectively

Metadata
You can find out why a shot is incorrectly exposed by checking its metadata. Open the underexposed image featured in step 1 – it's called Under.jpg, and you'll find it on the CD. Go to File > File Info, and in the dialog click on Camera Data 1. Here you'll discover that although the shot was taken with a wide aperture (f/5.6), the fast shutter speed of 1/400 sec meant that insufficient light was able to enter the camera.

Source files
This chapter is going to feature plenty of practical tonal-correction exercises using a variety of tools and techniques. All the problem images featured on this page will get a makeover; you'll find them on the CD, and once you've got the hang of the various tools you'll be able to use them to correct your own images.

1 Here's a typically underexposed shot. The blacks are too black, making detail hard to discern in the shadows and midtones, while the dull highlights lack detail and impact. We'll show you how to quickly improve this image using the Levels command on page 44.

2 This is a typically overexposed shot, produced by a wide aperture setting (f/5.6) and a relatively slow shutter speed (1/6 sec). Areas that should be dark look washed-out and weak, and the highlights are blown-out and lacking detail. We'll show you how to fix this shot so that it has a well-balanced tonal range on page 45.

3 Tricky lighting conditions have caused problems here. The building is backlit by a bright sky, creating a huge contrast between background and foreground. The photographer has exposed for the bright sky, causing foreground detail to be lost in the shadows and midtones. The Shadow/Highlight command can tackle this high-contrast challenge, as you'll see on page 52.

4 This image was taken in similar conditions to the previous shot, but this time the photographer has set the exposure to capture detail in the shadows and midtones, causing the detail in the sky to be burnt-out. On page 53 we'll show you how to restore maximum tonal detail to both the shadow and highlight areas.

Understanding histograms

Learn how to analyse an image's tonal range so that you can make the right adjustments

Histograms are invaluable tools when you're making exposure corrections, as they enable you to get a clear picture of an image's tonal range. By examining the histogram you can instantly see how pixels are distributed between the shadow, midtone and highlight areas, and identify where problems lie, enabling you to make effective corrections using the relevant tools. Below we'll show you how to read the histogram for a typical underexposed shot, and over the page we'll show you how to correct

You can get a clearer idea of this underexposed image's problems by studying its histogram: note how information is bunched at the left

the image, based on the information that the histogram provides, using the Levels dialog.

By the numbers
An image's darkest shadows will have an RGB value of or close to 0, and its brightest highlights a value of or close to 255. All other tones will have different combinations of RGB values, and where the three values are equal you get a pure grey. By altering these RGB levels you can change the tonal range of an image, and on the next few pages we'll show you how to put this theory into practice.

READING A HISTOGRAM

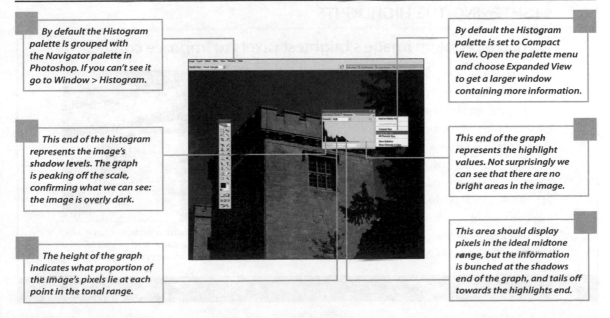

By default the Histogram palette is grouped with the Navigator palette in Photoshop. If you can't see it go to Window > Histogram.

This end of the histogram represents the image's shadow levels. The graph is peaking off the scale, confirming what we can see: the image is overly dark.

The height of the graph indicates what proportion of the image's pixels lie at each point in the tonal range.

By default the Histogram palette is set to Compact View. Open the palette menu and choose Expanded View to get a larger window containing more information.

This end of the graph represents the highlight values. Not surprisingly we can see that there are no bright areas in the image.

This area should display pixels in the ideal midtone range, but the information is bunched at the shadows end of the graph, and tails off towards the highlights end.

Fixing underexposure with Levels

You can quickly lighten an underexposed shot using the powerful Levels command

Having analysed an image's histogram to check its tonal range you can use the Levels dialog, which features its own built-in histogram, to correct the shot. In our underexposed image the brightest pixels have an RGB value of around 128, as they lie above the midtones slider in the centre of the histogram. You can lighten the highlight areas, and give the image a more evenly balanced tonal range, by remapping these pixels to a value of 255. Open the file Under.jpg from the CD, go to Image > Adjustments > Levels

The Levels dialog features a histogram similar to the one in the Histogram palette, and sliders that enable you to adjust a shot's tonal range

(Enhance > Adjust Lighting > Levels in Elements), and follow the steps below to brighten things up.

Output Levels

Much of our Levels editing involves changing the image's shadow and highlight Input Levels so that they correspond to the Output Levels of 0 for the shadows and 255 for the highlights. Don't alter the Output Levels – reducing the highlights Output Level from 255 would darken the entire image, including already dark areas, while increasing the shadows Output Level from 0 would lighten the image.

LIGHTENING THE HIGHLIGHTS

Remap a problem image's brightest pixels to improve contrast

To lighten our underexposed image's highlights click the white point Input Levels slider below the histogram, and drag it to the left until it meets the right-hand edge of the graph, which is where the brightest pixels in the image lie. These pixels will be remapped to pure white (255), and the rest of the highlights will be lightened accordingly – the reading in the right-hand Input Level field will change from 255 to 128, indicating that all pixels at level 128 have been mapped to level 255. When you adjust the white point slider the midtones slider (the grey one) is pushed to the left as well, which helps to brighten up the image's midtones.

A simple Levels adjustment has given the image a more even spread of shadows, midtones and highlights

Fixing overexposure with Levels

By targeting shadows instead of highlights you can restore dark tones to an overly-bright shot

The great thing about the Levels command is that you can diagnose and fix problems in a single interface, making it an efficient tool for performing tonal corrections. On the previous page we used the Levels sliders to rescue an extremely underexposed shot and make it usable – now let's tackle the typical overexposed shot that we introduced you to on page 42. Open Over.jpg from the CD. You can see straight away that there's too much highlight detail, and the shadows are washed-out; this time the histogram

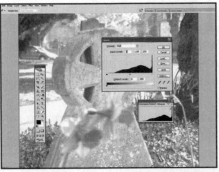

The information in this image's histogram is compressed in the midtones and highlights areas, and tails off towards the shadows end

information is bunched at the right of the graph, with no information in the darkest shadow areas.

Levels.mov
To see a demonstration of the Levels techniques outlined on these pages check out the video tutorial on the CD. You'll see just how easy it is to correct the tonal range and contrast of images suffering from both overexposure and underexposure.

DARKENING THE SHADOWS

A nudge of the black point Input Levels slider works wonders

To darken the shadow areas and expand the image's tonal range click the black point Input Levels slider, and drag it to the right until it meets the left-hand edge of the graph, which represents the darkest pixels in the image. This maps the image's darkest pixels to a pure black output level of 0, instead of their original value of 43. As with the white point slider, when you push the black point slider to the right the midtones slider will be pushed to the right as well. This has the effect of further darkening the darker midtone pixels in the image, which graduates the darkening effect and gives the image a nicely balanced tonal range.

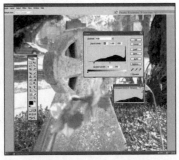

The Levels adjustment has mapped the image's darkest pixels to pure black, improving the contrast

Faster Levels adjustments

Improve an image's contrast even faster using the Levels eyedroppers and the Auto option

Levels eyedroppers
In Chapter 2 we showed you how to use the Levels eyedroppers to adjust an image's colour balance with a single click, and you can use the same tools to fix contrast problems just as quickly and effectively. Open Under.jpg, then open the Levels dialog and select the Set White Point eyedropper. Click in an area that should be white, and the tonal range of the entire image will be adjusted accordingly.

By now you should be getting a feel for how adjustments made with the Levels sliders remap a poorly exposed image's original tonal values to more appropriate shadow or highlight values. By remapping the brightest pixels in our underexposed image from 128 to 255 we brightened up the image dramatically, while remapping the darkest pixels in our underexposed image from 43 to 0 similarly improved that image's tonal range. Once you understand the concept of histograms and Levels you'll be able to quickly correct all manner of exposure-related problems.

As you'll see below you can also choose to have Photoshop correct an image automatically, and while this can be an easier option it's still useful to have a grasp of the basic theory. As with other automated adjustments it's good to know what's going on 'under the bonnet' when you use the Auto Levels options, as this will enable you to fine-tune things using the sliders if the adjustment doesn't produce the results you're looking for.

AUTO LEVELS

Use this option to improve tonal range and contrast in seconds

Now that you know how to adjust an image's levels manually, let's see how well the Auto Levels option works. Open the unedited version of Under.jpg, go to Image > Adjustments > Levels and click the Auto button. Photoshop will analyse the distribution of the image's shadow, midtone and highlight pixels, and change them so that the blacks are pure black (0) and the whites are pure white (255). You can tweak the Input Levels sliders to fine-tune the adjustment if necessary, but the results should be similar to our manual adjustment on page 44. The Auto option can work well, but there are some problems it can't fix, as you'll see on the facing page.

For general exposure corrections Auto Levels often does a decent job, although it does have its limitations

Missing midtones

The Auto Levels correction can't restore lost midtone detail, so you'll need to do it yourself

Open HighContrast.tif from the CD, and look at the Histogram palette: there's plenty of detail in the highlights, and information in the shadows, but there's a huge gap in the middle of the graph where the midtones should be represented. Go to Image > Adjustments > Levels. Clicking Auto would be ineffective, as Photoshop doesn't understand that you want to restore detail to the midtones of the silhouetted building. As far as it's concerned there's plenty of shadow and highlight information present at both ends of the graph, so

The huge gap in the middle of this image's histogram indicates an absence of midtones, and Auto Levels won't solve the problem

it makes virtually no alterations to the image. In situations like this you need to fix the problem yourself.

Precision editing
While the technique demonstrated on this page reveals detail lost in the shadows, it also tweaks an image's highlights, and, if the highlights were already correctly exposed, increasing the midtone levels can cause the highlights to become overexposed. Check out page 52 to see how you can target specific tonal problems more accurately, without affecting the image as a whole.

RESTORING MIDTONE DETAIL

Remap your midtones to bring out detail lost in the shadows

Open the Levels dialog, and click on the midtones Input Levels slider below the histogram (the grey slider). Bear in mind that Photoshop's tonal range is represented by the RGB scale of 0 (black) to 225 (pure white). The midtones slider is always initially at 128, which represents a midtone grey, although the value displayed is 1.00, to avoid confusion when the black and white points are adjusted (the midtone Input Levels value actually represents the gamma adjustment). Drag the slider to the left until the midtone value is approximately 2.75, and you'll now be able to see plenty of detail in the shadows.

Use the midtones Input Levels slider to lighten midtone areas, and reveal detail that was lost in the shadows

Curves

Use Curves to adjust specific areas of an image's tonal range without altering the rest of the shot

The Levels dialog enables you adjust shadows, midtones and highlights using three sliders, but if you want to target different tonal areas of your images more precisely you'll need to turn to Photoshop's Curves command (Curves isn't available in Elements). The dialog enables you to adjust an image by dragging points plotted on a curve (which is initially a straight line), and you can add as many points as you like, so you can tweak the levels of specific tones without affecting the rest of the image. Let's start by

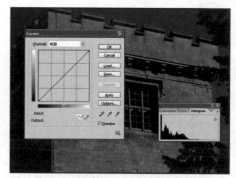

This shot's histogram indicates that there's little information in the highlights – a simple Curves adjustment will brighten things up

correcting our underexposed shot. Open Under.jpg again, and go to Image > Adjustment > Curves.

THE CURVES DIALOG

Drag the point you've placed upwards to set the Output level to nearer 255, and lighten the image.

This end of the curve represents the darkest pixels in the image.

To brighten up the image move the cursor to the middle of the curve, so that the level in the Input box reads around 128. Click to place a control point. (Note that the dashed line here represents the original line of the curve.)

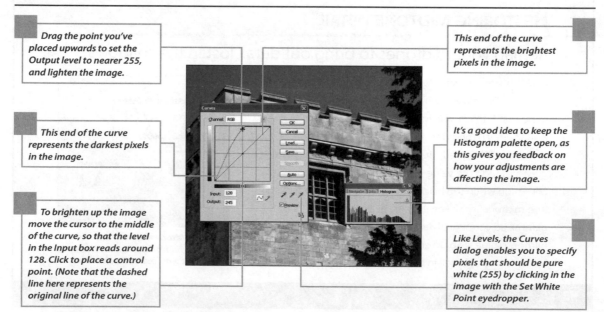

This end of the curve represents the brightest pixels in the image.

It's a good idea to keep the Histogram palette open, as this gives you feedback on how your adjustments are affecting the image.

Like Levels, the Curves dialog enables you to specify pixels that should be pure white (255) by clicking in the image with the Set White Point eyedropper.

Levels vs Curves

So which is the best tool for correcting the tonal range of an image – Levels or Curves?

Levels and Curves adjustments work in a similar way to alter an image's tonal range. Both tools enable you to remap an image's shadow or highlight input values to more appropriate output levels, and this enables you to use either tool to make shadow pixels darker or highlight pixels lighter. Both tools also enable you to remap an image's midtone pixels to give them a more appropriate output level, and both dialogs use the 0-255 RGB scale to represent tonal range. However, there are also some key differences

The Curves dialog gives you more control over your tonal corrections, but this flexibility also makes it easier to get things wrong

between the tools, and both have their strengths and weaknesses, as you'll see below.

Back to square one
If when working with the Curves dialog you find that you've placed too many control points, and are getting confused, click on any points you don't need and hit the [Backspace] key to delete them, or simply click and drag them out of the Curves window.

LEVELS BEST

The Curves dialog is certainly powerful, but simpler is often better

Because the Curves dialog enables you to use as many points as you want to adjust an image's tones it ought to be considered the most useful and powerful tool. However, its flexibility can actually be a disadvantage. Dragging one control point up or down to lighten or darken an image is simple enough, but if you start adding further points you can quickly end up with a complex curve that becomes hard to manage. The strength of the Levels dialog lies in its relative simplicity – the three control points for shadows, highlights and midtones should be enough to tackle the majority of tonal problems in your images.

Levels should be your first port of call for basic corrections: it's less complex than Curves, but just as effective

Avoiding clipping

The Levels dialog includes a tool that will help you to avoid clipping highlights and shadows

Gamut warning
The technique described below enables you to minimise clipping so that you can make more effective Levels adjustments. When you're tweaking tones you might also create colours that are outside the printable range. Open the View menu and click Gamut Warning: now, as you adjust your image, any out-of-gamut colours will be highlighted in grey, and you can fine-tune your adjustment accordingly.

When you use Curves or Levels to correct exposure you can sometimes introduce new problems. Adjusting an image's levels to lighten or darken areas can push some of the brightest or darkest pixels off the scale, and areas of pure white or pure black pixels that ought to contain detail are said to be clipped. You can spot clipping by looking at the edges of the histogram – visible tones will peak within the graph, but clipped tones will peak at the very edges. It can be hard to tell which pixels in an image

This shot (Brightness.jpg) is lacking highlight detail. You can boost the highlights without clipping using the technique described below

are clipped by looking at a graph, but the Levels dialog enables you to enable a visual clipping warning.

THRESHOLD MODE

Make more effective Levels adjustments without clipping detail

We touched on the concept of clipping back on page 31. Newer versions of the Adobe Camera Raw editor give you the option of displaying clipped highlights in red, and clipped shadows in blue, and you can then tweak your adjustments to avoid clipping. You can also see which pixels are close to being clipped while adjusting the white point or black point sliders in the Levels dialog. As you drag the sliders hold down [Alt]/[Option] to activate Threshold mode. You'll see areas of colour that change colour as pixels approach the point of clipping – this enables you to push your adjustments as far as possible without losing detail.

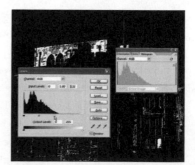

Hold down [Alt]/[Option] as you drag the white point or black point sliders to see a visual warning of clipping

The Brightness/Contrast dialog

You can use a simpler tonal adjustment tool to brighten up dull, underexposed shots fast

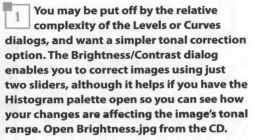

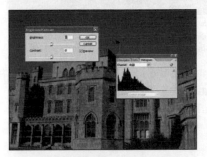

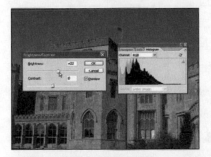

1 You may be put off by the relative complexity of the Levels or Curves dialogs, and want a simpler tonal correction option. The Brightness/Contrast dialog enables you to correct images using just two sliders, although it helps if you have the Histogram palette open so you can see how your changes are affecting the image's tonal range. Open Brightness.jpg from the CD.

2 You can see that this shot is badly underexposed, and lacks detail in the highlights. Look at the Histogram palette and you'll see that the information is bunched at the left of the graph, indicating that all the detail is in the shadow and midtone areas. You can use the Brightness/Contrast dialog to produce a correctly exposed version of the image.

3 Go to Image > Adjustments > Brightness/Contrast (Enhance > Adjust Lighting > Brightness/Contrast in Elements), and drag the Brightness slider to the right until the readout is +22 to lighten the image. The entire histogram will be shifted to the right, indicating increased brightness in the shadows, midtones and highlights.

4 To give the image a full tonal range that runs from pure black to pure white you need to stretch the histogram information so that it reaches both ends of the graph, and you can do this with the Contrast slider. For this image a value of +42 is enough to dramatically improve the tonal range and produce bright highlights, detailed midtones and strong shadows.

Helpful histogram
Without the histogram to guide you it would be difficult to use the Brightness/Contrast slider to create an image with healthy tonal range. The histogram enables you to see exactly how strong your image's shadows, midtones and highlights are – this helps you to redistribute the tones more effectively than if you were relying on your eye, and enables you to avoid clipping.

Camera histograms
Photoshop can fix most tonal problems, but the editing process does carry the risk of clipping, and of introducing artifacts such as picture noise. Some digital SLR cameras enable you to view a shot's histogram on the LCD monitor. This helps you to spot exposure problems at the time of capture, and gives you the opportunity to re-shoot the scene at a correct exposure.

Shadow/Highlight adjustments

You can target tonal problems more precisely using the Shadow/Highlight command

The Brightness/Contrast dialog is useful for dealing with tonal problems that affect an entire image. If an image is underexposed it can brighten up dull highlights and restore detail lost in the midtones and shadows, and it can also restore detail lost in the highlights of an overexposed shot to create a more balanced tonal range. However, it's not so good at targeting localised problems, such as those afflicting this image. The sky is correctly exposed, but the building is under-exposed, and is lacking detail; if you

The histogram for HighContrast.tif, which you'll find on the CD, has a gap in the middle indicating missing midtone information – we'll fix it below

lightened the image to reveal that detail using Brightness/Contrast you would overexpose the sky.

THE SHADOW/HIGHLIGHT INTERFACE

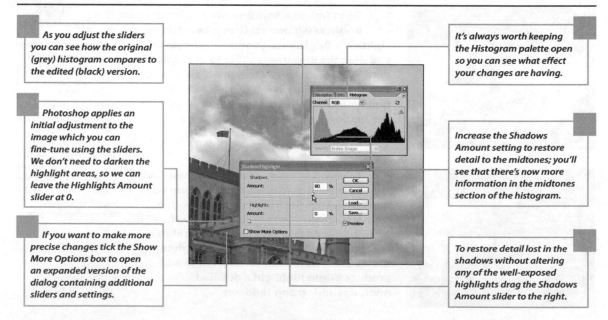

As you adjust the sliders you can see how the original (grey) histogram compares to the edited (black) version.

Photoshop applies an initial adjustment to the image which you can fine-tune using the sliders. We don't need to darken the highlight areas, so we can leave the Highlights Amount slider at 0.

If you want to make more precise changes tick the Show More Options box to open an expanded version of the dialog containing additional sliders and settings.

It's always worth keeping the Histogram palette open so you can see what effect your changes are having.

Increase the Shadows Amount setting to restore detail to the midtones; you'll see that there's now more information in the midtones section of the histogram.

To restore detail lost in the shadows without altering any of the well-exposed highlights drag the Shadows Amount slider to the right.

Advanced Shadow/Highlight

Make more precise corrections by adjusting the additional sliders in the expanded dialog

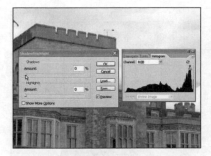

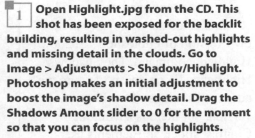

1 **Open Highlight.jpg from the CD. This shot has been exposed for the backlit building, resulting in washed-out highlights and missing detail in the clouds. Go to Image > Adjustments > Shadow/Highlight. Photoshop makes an initial adjustment to boost the image's shadow detail. Drag the Shadows Amount slider to 0 for the moment so that you can focus on the highlights.**

Radius sliders

We've avoided touching the Radius sliders, as this can add unwanted artifacts to images. The Radius setting determines the size of the area around each pixel that's analysed to determine whether a pixel is in the shadows or highlights; if you reduce the Highlights Radius slider to around 6 pixels, for example, you'll create a white halo around the outline of the building. The default Radius settings are fine for most corrections.

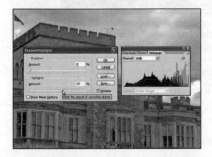

2 **Drag the Highlights Amount slider to 57% – you'll see more detail appear in the sky's highlights and midtones. However, since the building also consists mainly of midtones it too has been altered, and now looks rather washed-out, with reduced contrast. It's time to go 'under the bonnet', and tinker with the Shadow/Highlight dialog's more advanced options.**

3 **Tick Show More Options, and the dialog will expand to reveal more controls. Go to the Highlights section, and drag the Tonal Width slider to the left until you reach 14% – this limits the Highlights adjustment to a narrower tonal width, so that it adds detail to the sky while preserving the midtones of the building.**

Extra impact

The Color Correction slider only boosts colours in areas that have been altered using the other sliders, and it doesn't have much effect on most of our image's washed-out colours. However, the image can be greatly improved by boosting the intensity of all its colours. After completing step 4, click OK to apply the Shadow/Highlight adjustments, then go to Image > Adjustments > Hue/Saturation. Choose Master from the Edit menu, and drag the Saturation slider up to +18 to create colours with more impact.

4 **You can improve the contrast of the building's flat-lit midtones using the Adjustments section of the expanded dialog. Drag the Midtone Contrast slider up to +30, then go back to the Shadows section and boost the Amount slider to 19%. Follow the tip in the 'Extra impact' sidebar to add more punch to the image's drab colours.**

Tonal correction in Elements

For a simple approach to balancing an image's tonal range try Elements 4's Quick Fix mode

Auto limitations
You'll notice that the Quick Fix interface also has Auto Levels and Auto Contrast buttons in the Lighting section, but neither of these will correct the problems of ShadowHighlight.jpg. This is because the histogram displays plenty of detail at both the shadow and highlight ends of the graph, and Elements isn't intelligent enough to realise that you want to bring out detail in the midtone shadow areas.

As we mentioned on page 52, Elements 4 users have their own version of Photoshop's Shadow/ Highlight command. The Shadows/ Highlights dialog doesn't feature the advanced settings of the Photoshop version, but there is a Midtone Contrast slider, so Elements users can target midtone pixels without altering correctly exposed areas. Open ShadowHighlight.jpg – you'll see that the grass is underexposed, but the sky has plenty of detail. Go to Enhance > Adjust Lighting > Shadows/Highlights, and drag the

The original shot is on the right and the edited shot is on the left – you can see how we've brought out detail that was lost in the shadows

Lighten Shadows slider up to 43% to lighten the grass. Alternatively, use the Quick Fix interface (see below).

QUICK FIX TONAL CORRECTIONS

The Lighting section provides all the tools you need to adjust problems caused by incorrect exposure.

The image has been exposed to capture detail in the bright cloudy sky, causing foreground detail to be lost in the underexposed shadows.

The Before and After view option makes it easy to compare your corrected image with the original.

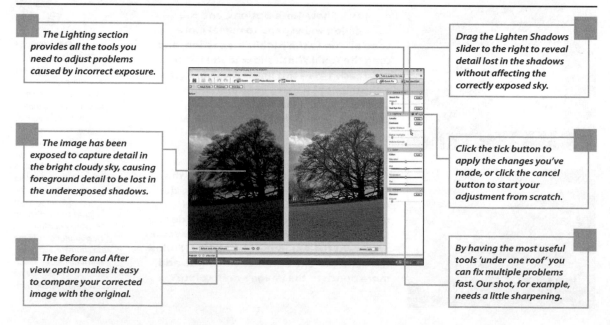

Drag the Lighten Shadows slider to the right to reveal detail lost in the shadows without affecting the correctly exposed sky.

Click the tick button to apply the changes you've made, or click the cancel button to start your adjustment from scratch.

By having the most useful tools 'under one roof' you can fix multiple problems fast. Our shot, for example, needs a little sharpening.

Auto Smart Fix

This Elements 4 tool can do an even better job of correcting tonal problems than Auto Levels

This chapter started out by looking at how you can tackle different tonal problems manually using a variety of tools in Photoshop and Elements. You've learned how to read a histogram to get a better idea of the tonal range of an image, and understanding histograms is important, as they enable you to step in when the Auto correction tools fail to produce the desired results. Often, the Auto options will do a perfectly good job, and Auto Levels works well on shots that are underexposed or overexposed. If the image's histogram has little or no information at either the highlights or shadows end of the graph, Auto Levels adjusts the image to introduce information across the entire tonal range. However, we've also seen that Auto Levels isn't smart enough to know when you want to restore lost midtone information. The Shadow/Highlight command in Photoshop and Elements is an effective way of correcting such images, but Elements 4 boasts an even smarter tool that can improve the shots Auto Levels can't: Auto Smart Fix.

More detail
Auto Smart Fix works well on underexposed shots such as Under.jpg. On page 40 we used Levels to give this dull shot a healthier tonal range, creating a brighter, bluer sky and adding more detail to the building's highlights while preserving the shadows. Auto Smart Fix also restores detail to the highlights, and in addition boosts details lost in the darkest shadows that weren't visible after our manual Levels adjustment.

AUTO SMART FIX

Correct tonal problems in seconds using this Quick Fix option

Auto Smart Fix can take a while to work its magic, but it often succeeds where Auto Levels and Auto Contrast fail. As well as remapping pixels' tonal values to create strong blacks and bright whites, the adjustment also improves midtone levels. Auto Smart Fix combines the power of Elements' Shadows/Highlights sliders and Auto Levels to bring out detail in the shadows, midtones and highlights, and it also beefs-up the image's colours. Open HighContrast.jpg in Quick Fix mode, and click the Auto button next to the Smart Fix slider to correct your image. You can also use the slider to adjust an image manually, or to fine-tune the Auto correction.

Auto Smart Fix reaches the problem pixels Auto Levels can't, and restores colour and detail throughout a shot

Combining exposures

Combine two differently exposed photos to create a shot with a well-balanced tonal range

Auto Bracketing
An easy way to capture differently exposed versions of the same scene is to use your camera's Auto Bracketing function, if it has one. The camera will adjust the shutter speed to take shots one f-stop over and one f-stop under the optimum exposure setting. Make sure the camera is set to aperture priority to maintain the same depth of field in each shot.

When you edit an image using the tools featured in this chapter you run the risk of adding artifacts to the shot; these can range from increased picture noise to dramatic halos around areas of high contrast. When you're faced with difficult lighting conditions a good way of minimising editing is to take two differently exposed shots of a scene and combine them. In our example the camera is first set to expose for the bright sky, and then to capture shadow detail in the grass and trees. Using the techniques on

The shot on the left was exposed to capture the colour and detail in the sky, and the shot on the right was exposed for the grass and trees

the facing page you can combine the images to create a tonally balanced and relatively artifact-free shot.

DOUBLE EXPOSURE

Capture two identically framed shots with different exposures

In order for the technique outline on the facing page to work the two shots need to be framed identically. Place your camera on a tripod and compose your image. Take an exposure reading for the sky, and press the shutter to capture a shot with the maximum amount of colour and detail in the sky (use a remote trigger if you have one to ensure that you don't move the camera). Then reduce the shutter speed, and take a longer exposure to capture the colour and detail in the landscape. Neither of these shots is ideal, but by combining them you can create a single shot that has correctly exposed highlights and shadows.

On the facing page we'll combine the two shots shown above to create this perfectly exposed image

Two into one

Use layers, a layer mask and the Gradient Tool to blend the differently exposed shots together

1 Open Sky.jpg and Ground.jpg from the CD. Sky.jpg was exposed to capture the bright sky, and as a result the ground and trees are underexposed; Ground.jpg was exposed to capture detail in the landscape, causing the sky to be overexposed. Select Ground.jpg and go to Select > All, then copy and paste this file into Sky.jpg as a new layer. Label the layers Sky and Ground.

2 Select the Ground layer, and click the 'Add a mask' icon in the Layers palette. A white mask thumbnail will appear next to the layer thumbnail. Select the Gradient Tool (G), and hit D to make the foreground and background colours white and black (the default mask colours). Select Linear Gradient in the options bar, and Foreground to Background from the Gradient Picker.

3 Click the layer mask thumbnail to select the mask, then draw a short vertical line roughly in the centre of the image to create a white-to-black gradient. The lower white area will preserve the correctly exposed grass and trees, and the upper black area will make the overexposed sky become transparent, revealing the correctly exposed sky from the layer below.

4 The grass and sky now look correctly exposed, but some of the trees will also have been revealed, and will look too dark. Select a soft brush, and carefully paint with the white foreground colour on the mask to reveal the lighter trees on the Ground layer; if you accidentally reveal any of the overexposed sky switch to a black brush to restore the correctly exposed sky.

Combine.mov
Check out the video tutorial on the CD to see this technique demonstrated. You'll see just how easy it is to use the Gradient Tool, a layer mask and brushes to reveal the best areas of two source images. Note that Elements doesn't include the layer masks feature, but if you're using Elements you can use a soft-edged Eraser Tool set to varying opacities to erase parts of the Ground layer and reveal the Sky layer below.

Aligning images
If you don't have a tripod you'll need to align your images manually (unless you have a very steady hand!). Set your camera to Auto Bracketing as explained on the facing page to capture similarly composed pictures. When you open the images in Photoshop, if they're not perfectly aligned reduce the opacity of the foreground layer so you can see the layer below, and align the shots using the Move Tool (V). To move the foreground layer in small increments use the arrow keys.

Gradient effects

Enhance a landscape image by using the Gradient Tool to create dramatic beams of light

Saving gradients
After you've tinkered with the Gradient Editor to create your light beam effect, as shown on the facing page, you'll be able to save the gradient to use again. Click on the Save button in the Gradient Editor, and label the gradient 'Light Beams'.

You can use Photoshop's tools to do much more than just correct your images. On the previous page we used the Gradient Tool as a masking tool, and blended two shots together to create an image with a balanced exposure. The Gradient Tool can also be used as a painting tool, and by digging deeper into the Gradient Editor you can modify the tool to add all kinds of effects to your shots. Below we'll take you on a guided tour of the Gradient Editor, and on the facing page we'll show you how to use the

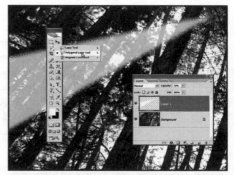

A feathered Polygonal Lasso selection can be used to create an effective light beam, but the technique is too slow for adding multiple beams

Gradient Tool to create dramatic beams of sunlight bursting through the canopy of a dark forest.

THE GRADIENT TOOL AND GRADIENT EDITOR

Click these icons to specify the type of gradient that will be drawn. By default the tool draws a linear gradient, but we'll be using the Angle option in our walkthrough.

This preview shows what the selected gradient will look like. Click the adjacent button to open the Gradient Picker and choose a different preset, or click the preview to open the Gradient Editor if you want to edit the gradient.

The Gradient Tool (G) shares a compartment with the Paint Bucket Tool.

These presets are the same as those in the Gradient Picker, and enable you to change the default gradient.

The Gradient Type menu enables you to choose between a regular gradient and a noise-based effect – we'll be using the latter option in the walkthrough.

The colours of a gradient are defined by colour stops. You can add more colour stops to alter the look of the gradient, and the preview will update to reflect any changes you make.

Creating light beams

We'll start by configuring a custom gradient that will form the basis of our light rays effect

1 Open Forest.jpg from the CD, and select the Gradient Tool (G). Open the Gradient Editor, choose the Foreground to Background preset, and choose Noise from the Gradient Type menu to create a gradient made up of vertical bands of colour. These bands of colour will form our light beams.

2 To exaggerate the bands of colour change the Roughness value to 100%, and to create the effect of separate beams tick the Add Transparency box at the bottom-right of the dialog. If you want to save the gradient see the sidebar on the facing page.

3 Click OK to apply the changes. You'll notice that the gradient preview in the options bar changes to show the gradient you've created. Click the Angle Gradient button – it's the middle of the five icons next to the gradient preview. Go to the Layers palette, click the 'Create a new layer' icon and label the layer 'Light Rays'.

4 Click somewhere in the top-right of the image (but not too close to the edges) and drag to draw a gradient. At this stage the colours are too garish and the light beams are too sharp; on the next page you'll use a filter effect and layer blending modes to create more realistic beams.

Forest.jpg
We've included the source image used in this walkthrough on the CD so that you can create this effect for yourself. Once you've mastered the technique you can adapt It to enhance your own shots – you could, for example, create beams of light streaming in through a church window.

Which is which?
The five gradient style icons in the options bar don't give you a particularly clear indication of what the various styles are. To find out which gradient is which hover your cursor over each one in turn; assuming you haven't disabled the tooltips option in Preferences the names of the gradients will be displayed.

Creating light beams continued

Complete the effect by turning your coloured light beams into more subtle white rays

Brighter beams
To give your light beams more impact, duplicate the Light Rays layer by dragging it on to the 'Create a new layer' icon. Alternatively, increase the layer's opacity to around 80%, or whatever's appropriate if you're using a different background image.

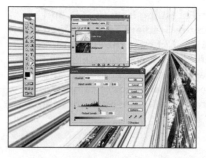

5 Still in the Light Rays layer, go to Image > Adjustments > Desaturate to remove the colour from the beams. To turn the grey beams white go to Image > Adjustments > Levels, and drag the white point Input Levels slider to the left until the reading is around 130. Click OK to apply the adjustment.

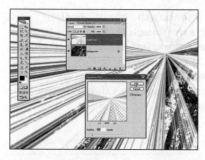

6 To give the beams a softer, feathered edge go to Filter > Blur > Gaussian Blur; a Radius setting of around 1.8 pixels should do the trick. Click OK to apply the filter.

Light Rays.mov
There are quite a few steps involved in creating our light ray effect, and some of the techniques are fairly involved, especially if you're relatively new to Photoshop. Check out the video tutorial on the CD to see exactly what's going on at each stage of the process.

7 You may find that some black beams of 'light' are still visible. To remove them set the layer's blending mode to Screen, so that only the white beams will be visible. For a more subtle effect reduce the layer's opacity setting to around 55%. The beam effect is a little over the top at this stage, but you can make it more subtle by drawing another gradient on a layer mask.

8 Click the 'Add a mask' icon at the foot of the Layers palette, and target the mask. Select the Gradient Tool again, choose the default Foreground to Background preset, and Draw a Linear gradient on the mask to make the beams fade out. Elements users can fade parts of the Light Rays layer using a soft Eraser Tool, or create a Gradient adjustment layer in step 1 and edit that.

Gradient rainbows

Enhance a dull landscape shot by adapting a gradient preset to spectacular effect

Nature is a great source of awe-inspiring subject matter, but we're usually dependent on the right conditions, and a big slice of luck in terms of being in the right place at the right time to capture rare events such as a lightning bolt hitting a photogenic location. However, with the right know-how you can use Photoshop's tools to add all sorts of scene-enhancing natural effects to your photos. Rainbows are another natural phenomenon that's hard to capture on camera, and you can use the Gradient Tool to add a

This photo has a large, bland area of sky that can be made more interesting with the addition of a Photoshop-created rainbow

realistic-looking rainbow to any image in a few simple steps – we'll show you how below.

Finishing touches
Once you're happy with the shape and position of your rainbow set the layer's blending mode to Screen so that you can see the landscape through the rainbow, and reduce the opacity of the layer. You can adapt the layer mask techniques used previously to make your rainbow fade gently away, or use a soft-edged Eraser Tool set to a low opacity.

CREATING A RAINBOW

Add a rainbow to any landscape photo – whatever the weather!

Open Rainbow.jpg from the CD and create a new layer. Select the Gradient Tool (G), and open the Gradient Editor. In the Presets section click Transparent Rainbow to select it, and click OK. Go to the options bar, make sure the Transparency option is enabled, and click the Linear Gradient button. Draw a short horizontal line in the middle of the image to create a vertical rainbow. To bend the rainbow go to Filter > Distort > Shear, place a control point in the centre of the line and drag it to the right. To place the rainbow the right way up go to Edit > Transform > Rotate 90° CCW. CS2 users can use the Transform > Warp command to bend the rainbow.

By distorting and transforming a gradient you can see a rainbow whenever you like!

CREATING AND MODIFYING SELECTIONS

You can use a number of different tools to isolate specific pixels in an image for editing. We'll explain which tool to use, and show you how you can quickly create perfect selections

When you're editing images you'll often want to make changes to a specific part of a shot, or edit a specific range of colours, without altering the rest of the image. You might, for example, want to isolate the pixels that make up a bland sky so that you can replace them with a more dramatic skyscape; or extract a person from a photograph so that you can move them their original surroundings to somewhere more interesting. Or you might simply want to change the colour of an object, such as a car without altering the background colours in the image. When deciding which tool to use to make a certain

selection, you're spoiled for choice. Both Photoshop and Elements have several tools to do this and deciding which one to use can be more tricky than actually making the selection!

The right tool

When faced with selecting a sky, for example, you might automatically reach for Magic Wand Tool; it will often do the job, but you might find that the Color Range dialog enables you to make an effective selection more quickly, thanks to its ability to provide visual feedback regarding the selected pixels. Likewise, you could cut out a complex figure using the Lasso Tool, but you'll make

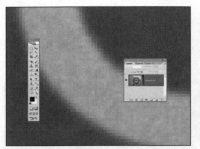

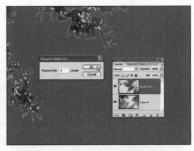

Page 64 *Make quick selections around simple shapes with the Marquee tools*

Page 66 *You can create a rough selection in seconds with the Lasso Tool*

Page 69 *Modify a Magic Wand Tool selection to remove colour fringes*

Page 70 *Make complex colour-based selections with the Color Range dialog*

Page 73 *Select complex outlines easily with Elements' Magic Extractor dialog*

Page 87 *Modify a selection to turn a daytime shot into a stunning silhouette*

faster progress, and create a more accurate selection to boot, using the Magnetic Lasso. And, while you may be tempted to use the Magnetic Lasso to select an object such as a sailing boat, you'll find that the Pen Tool's editable Bezier curves will enable you to select the boat's flowing lines more easily.

Modifying selections

Once you've used a selection tool to isolate an area or range of pixels, you can edit, feather and otherwise fine-tune the selection in a number of ways to make it perfect. We'll show you how to use Quick Mask mode to quickly tidy up your selections, and you'll discover how to turn a temporary selection into a layer mask, so that you can fine-tune it at your leisure. We'll also show you how to store Pen Tool selections as permanent paths, so that you can reactivate the selection and edit it at any time in the future.

Elements 4 includes a couple of unique selection tools, and we'll show you how to get the best out of those too. By the end of this chapter you'll find that you're able to analyse even the most daunting of selection challenges, reach for the most appropriate tool, and isolate the pixels that you want to work on with the minimum of effort.

The Marquee tools

We'll introduce you to the concept of selections by looking at how the simplest tools work

Digital mosaics
Photoshop's pixels work on the same principle as a mosaic. Mosaics are made up of many coloured tiles, which, when viewed from a distance, make up an image. Like these tiles each pixel has a single colour, but when they're reduced to a microscopic size on your monitor they produce smooth graduations of tone and colour.

W hen you open an image in Photoshop and zoom right in, you'll see that it's made up of thousands of tiny coloured squares. These are called pixels (short for picture elements), and they're the building blocks that make up your shots. At normal magnification they create an effective illusion of reality, and by selecting and manipulating these pixels you can alter the reality of an image in a convincing way. Photoshop and Elements have no shortage of tools to help you make selections, and the simplest of these

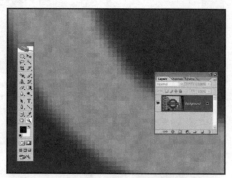

At full magnification you can see that a digital photo is made up of thousands of tiny blocks of colour called pixels

are the Marquee tools. Check the box below for an introduction to the tools, and to selections in general.

MARQUEES AND SELECTIONS

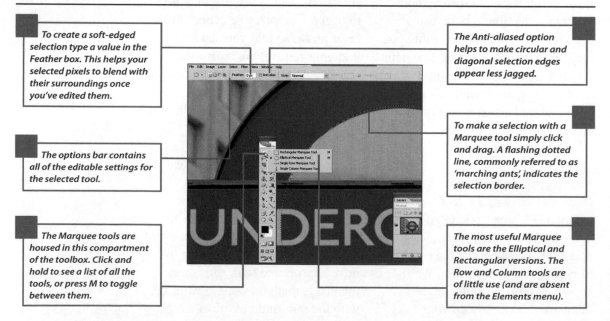

To create a soft-edged selection type a value in the Feather box. This helps your selected pixels to blend with their surroundings once you've edited them.

The options bar contains all of the editable settings for the selected tool.

The Marquee tools are housed in this compartment of the toolbox. Click and hold to see a list of all the tools, or press M to toggle between them.

The Anti-aliased option helps to make circular and diagonal selection edges appear less jagged.

To make a selection with a Marquee tool simply click and drag. A flashing dotted line, commonly referred to as 'marching ants', indicates the selection border.

The most useful Marquee tools are the Elliptical and Rectangular versions. The Row and Column tools are of little use (and are absent from the Elements menu).

Marquee selections

Combine the Elliptical and Rectangular tools to create more complex selection marquees

1 Open Sign.jpg. You'll use the Elliptical and Rectangular Marquee tools to select the main sign so that you can make it stand out from its background. As the sign was photographed head-on, the Marquee tools offer the quickest way of selecting it. We could also use the Magnetic Lasso, but that would take longer. Start by selecting the Elliptical Marquee Tool (M).

2 Go to the options bar, and set Feather to 2 pixels – this will create a more gentle blend between the selected area and the rest of the image. Click in the centre of the circular sign and drag outwards; to make the circle emanate from the central point hold down [Alt]/[Option], and to draw a perfect circle press [Shift]. See the sidebars for tips on fine-tuning the selection.

3 Hit M again to select the Rectangular Marquee Tool. By default when you draw a new selection it will replace any existing selections, so go the options bar and click the 'Add to selection' button. Draw a selection around the rectangular part of the sign; this will be combined with your circular selection, and the whole sign will be selected.

4 With the selection marquee still active click the 'Create new fill or adjustment layer' button in the Layers palette, and choose Levels. The adjustment layer's mask will be based on your selection. In the Levels dialog brighten the highlights by pushing the white point Input Levels slider to around 205. The selected sign will be brightened, and the background will be unaffected.

Fine-tuning selections
If your Elliptical Marquee Tool selection isn't perfect, right-click inside the selection and choose Transform Selection from the context menu – a bounding box will appear around the selection, and you can click and drag the handles to adjust the scale and shape of the selection. If you right-click again with the bounding box active you'll see a menu of transformation options that you can apply.

Transform options
When you right-click to open the first menu referred to above, make sure you choose Transform Selection and not Free Transform – if you choose the latter option the pixels you've selected will be transformed, rather than the selection marquee, and the size of the sign will be altered. However, once you've chosen Transform Selection, when you right-click again to call up the second context menu, the Free Transform option listed there will be applied to the selection, not the pixels. You can also use the directional arrow keys to nudge your selection into position.

The Lasso tools

If an object's outline is too complicated to select with one of the Marquee tools, lasso it!

Quick swap

You can combine the Lasso Tool and the Polygonal Lasso to make selections. When you're using the Lasso Tool, temporarily switch to the Polygonal Lasso by holding down [Alt]/[Option], then releasing the mouse and clicking to draw straight lines. Release the [Alt]/[Option] key to revert to the Lasso Tool. If you're starting out with the Polygonal Lasso, holding down [Alt]/[Option] will switch you to the Lasso Tool.

You'll find the Lasso tools (L) directly beneath the Marquee tools in the Photoshop toolbox, and to the right of the Marquee tools in Elements 4. The Lasso Tool is the most basic of the three tools, and enables you to draw a quick freehand selection, which is fine if you only want to make a 'rough and ready' selection. You simply click and hold the mouse button, then draw with the tool to make a selection, and when you release the mouse button the selection will be completed. Two more useful Lasso

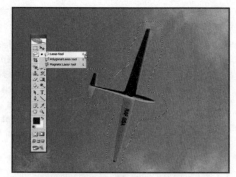

The basic Lasso Tool is perfect for making 'rough and ready' selections where accuracy isn't essential

tools are the Polygonal Lasso, which we'll take a look at below, and the Magnetic Lasso, featured opposite.

THE POLYGONAL LASSO TOOL

This tool enables you to select straight-edged objects easily

The Polygonal Lasso Tool enables you to select straight-edged objects in seconds by simply clicking on the corner points to draw straight lines. When you get close to the first point that you placed a small circle will appear next to the cursor, indicating that the next click will close the selection; click and you'll see the 'marching ants' border appear. In addition to selecting irregular straight-edged objects, such as the roof of a house, the Polygonal Lasso Tool can also be used to select distorted square or rectangular shapes that the Rectangular Marquee Tool wouldn't be able to select, such as a picture frame shot from an angle.

You can make rectangular or polygonal selections quickly and effectively with the Polygonal Lasso

handwritten notes: LASSO - 10, H-9%, S-79%, A-0%, R-100%

The Magnetic Lasso Tool

Select complicated shapes with the minimum of effort using the amazing Magnetic Lasso

The Marquee tools are great for selecting simple shapes, and the Polygonal Lasso happily tackles straight-edged objects, but none of these tools are capable of selecting complicated shapes such as a person. If you want to cut out a figure from one image so that you can add them to another you'll need a tool that's up to the job, and that tool is the Magnetic Lasso. It combines the freehand drawing feature of the Lasso Tool with the anchor point feature of the Polygonal Lasso Tool, enabling you to create complex

Isolating a figure from their background is a common task If you're creating composite images – the Magnetic Lasso makes it easy

selections quickly and accurately. Check out the annotated image below to see how to use the tool.

Deleting points
If the Magnetic Lasso Tool gets lost when placing its anchor points automatically feel free to make the occasional mouse click to place a point manually. If the tool places a point in the wrong place (or you do!) hit [Backspace] to delete it; you can delete as many points as you want until you get to the last point that was correctly placed, and then carry on making your selection.

MAGNETIC LASSO

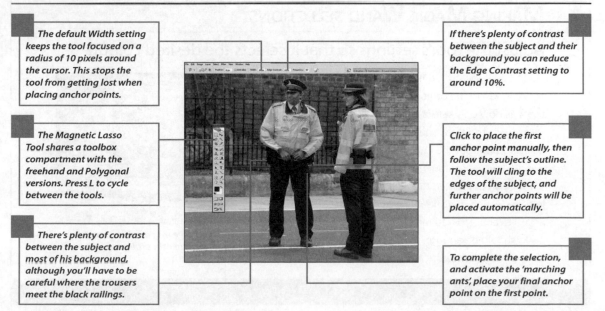

The default Width setting keeps the tool focused on a radius of 10 pixels around the cursor. This stops the tool from getting lost when placing anchor points.

The Magnetic Lasso Tool shares a toolbox compartment with the freehand and Polygonal versions. Press L to cycle between the tools.

There's plenty of contrast between the subject and most of his background, although you'll have to be careful where the trousers meet the black railings.

If there's plenty of contrast between the subject and their background you can reduce the Edge Contrast setting to around 10%.

Click to place the first anchor point manually, then follow the subject's outline. The tool will cling to the edges of the subject, and further anchor points will be placed automatically.

To complete the selection, and activate the 'marching ants', place your final anchor point on the first point.

The Magic Wand Tool

If you want to select colours, rather than shapes, you need a different kind of tool

Pasting into selections
To paste another image into the selected area, open any file (or use Inset.jpg from the disc) and choose Select > All, then Edit > Copy. Go back to the phone image, make sure the selection is active, and choose Edit > Paste Into to paste the image into the selection as a new layer. Reduce the opacity of the new layer to 70% to blend the photo and the phone screen's darker pixels together more realistically.

To demonstrate how the Magic Wand Tool works we're going to select the pixels that make up a mobile phone's screen so that we can replace them with a photo. The Rectangular Marquee Tool wouldn't be able to select the screen's curved edges, and, while we could use the Magnetic Lasso Tool, as there's plenty of contrast between the black screen and the silver phone, there's an even faster option. Because the screen is made up of similarly coloured pixels the Magic Wand Tool (W) is the best candidate for

Because this phone's dark screen is made up of similarly coloured pixels we can use the Magic Wand Tool to select them

the job, as it can make a colour-based selection in seconds – see below for a guide to using it.

MAKING MAGIC WAND SELECTIONS

Adjust the tool's settings so that it selects the desired colours

Open Magic.jpg from the CD, and select the Magic Wand Tool (W). Go to the options bar and tick Contiguous: the tool will now only select similarly coloured pixels that are adjacent to the areas you click on, rather than selecting pixels throughout the entire image. To make the tool select a wider range of colours increase the Tolerance setting to 55. Click on the screen to start making the selection, and an initial selection marquee will be created. Hold down [Shift] and click again to add more pixels to the marquee – three clicks should be enough to select the entire phone screen, and you can then paste another image into the selection.

Once you've made a selection you can, among other things, paste an image into it

Modifying selections

You can adjust the Magic Wand's marquee to remove colour fringes from unselected areas

1 The Magic Wand Tool can be used to make more complex selections with the help of the modification options in the Select menu. Open SkyReplacement.jpg. You'll use the Magic Wand to select the dull sky so that you can replace it. The challenge is to capture the tiny areas of sky among the leaves but without selecting the details of the branches and leaves themselves.

2 Select the Magic Wand Tool and turn off the Contiguous option so that the tool will select pixels throughout the image. Click to sample the white sky. You'll see the 'marching ants' appear around the edges of the building and the branches, but they'll also appear around the lighter parts of the building, so resample the sky using a lower Tolerance setting of around 6.

3 Double-click the Background layer's thumbnail in the Layers palette to unlock it, and hit [Backspace] to replace the white sky with a transparent background. Create a new layer called Blue Sky, and Edit > Fill the selection on the new layer with blue. Hit [Ctrl]/[Command]+H to hide the marquee and you'll see that there are still some white pixels clinging to the edges of the leaves.

4 Press [Ctrl]/[Command]+H again to reveal the selection marquee. Go to Select > Modify > Expand, and type in a value of 1 pixel. The entire marquee will expanded by a single pixel, adding the fringes of white to the selected area. Edit > Fill the modified selection with blue, and the fringe around the building and the leaves will disappear.

Other modifications
In this walkthrough we show you how to expand a selection marquee so that it removes an unwanted fringe of colour. You can also shrink a selection, by going to Select > Modify > Contract, and the Modify sub-menu also includes a Smooth option, which cleans up stray pixels inside or outside a selection, and a Border option, which softens the edges of a selection by adding an anti-aliased border around it.

Defringe in Elements
Elements has the Select > Modify options, but it also boasts a dedicated fringe-removal tool. Once you've deleted the white sky, deselect the marquee by going to Select > Deselect, or by hitting [Ctrl]/ [Command]+D. Go to Enhance > Adjust Color > Defringe Layer, and type a value in the Width field.

Color Range selections

Create a colour-based selection with more accuracy using this sophisticated command

Different shades
Selecting all the shades of red in these phone boxes is a tough job, as the pixels vary in tone between areas of sunlight and shadow. The extra level of control and feedback that the Color Range dialog gives you makes it the best choice for challenging selection jobs such as this.

The Magic Wand Tool enables you to quickly select pixels of a similar colour. However, the tool can sometimes fail to select every pixel you want, as some pixels may fall just outside the specified range, and you can easily miss a small cluster of 'marching ants' tucked away in the corner of the image that indicates unselected pixels. Another tool that makes selections based on colour is the Color Range command. The advantage this tool has over the Magic Wand is that it gives you more visual feedback regarding your

The varying hues of red make selecting these phone boxes with the Magic Wand Tool tricky; the Color Range command can do a better job

selection, and it's also easier to fine-tune the selection to capture all the pixels you want.

THE COLOR RANGE INTERFACE

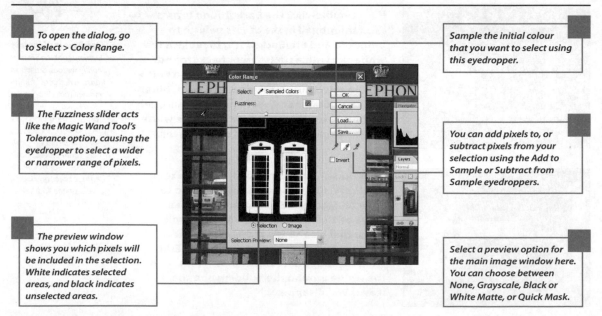

To open the dialog, go to Select > Color Range.

The Fuzziness slider acts like the Magic Wand Tool's Tolerance option, causing the eyedropper to select a wider or narrower range of pixels.

The preview window shows you which pixels will be included in the selection. White indicates selected areas, and black indicates unselected areas.

Sample the initial colour that you want to select using this eyedropper.

You can add pixels to, or subtract pixels from your selection using the Add to Sample or Subtract from Sample eyedroppers.

Select a preview option for the main image window here. You can choose between None, Grayscale, Black or White Matte, or Quick Mask.

Color Range in action

We can select the many different tones of red in these phone boxes with just a few clicks

1 Open Phonebooth.jpg from the CD, and go to Select > Color Range to open the Color Range dialog. Select the Eyedropper Tool (the left of the three eyedroppers), and click in a dark red area to sample that shade. The sampled colour will appear as the foreground colour in the toolbox, and pixels of a similar value will show up in the preview window as white or grey.

2 To select a wider range of red pixels increase the Fuzziness slider to around 100. More of the grey areas in the preview window will turn white, indicating that you've selected more of the red pixels. The lighter red pixels will remain grey, meaning that they're only partially selected.

3 To add the rest of the red pixels to the selection choose the Add to Sample eyedropper. Click on a light red area at the top of one of the phone boxes in the main image, or click on a corresponding grey area in the preview window. Tweak the Fuzziness slider until the desired pixels are pure white, and the rest of the preview is black.

4 When you're happy with your selection click OK, and the familiar 'marching ants' marquee will appear in the main image window. You can now edit the selected area, for example by changing the colours using a Hue/Saturation adjustment.

ColorRange.mov
We'll take you through the walkthrough on this page in our video tutorial. You'll be able to see just how effective the Color Range command is at selecting pixels of a similar colour, even when some areas are in light and others in shade.

Fuzziness
You may need to experiment with a different Fuzziness value to the one we've used, as it's unlikely that you'll sample the exact same pixels that we did using the eyedropper. Take as many samples as you need, and if you decide you want to start from scratch hold down [Alt]/[Option] to change the Cancel button to Reset, and click the button.

The Extract Filter

Photoshop's Extract Filter makes it easy to select objects with highly detailed edges

Extract.jpg
You can practise using the Extract filter to select a complex shape by using our source file on the CD. By way of comparison, try using the Magnetic Lasso to select the dog – you'll find that you won't be able to select as much outline detail.

We've seen that the Magnetic Lasso Tool can do a pretty good job of selecting subjects with complex outlines. However, the tool can get into trouble when faced with detailed edges such as hair or fur, and even if you manage to cut your subject out you're likely to end up with a jagged outline, which will be noticeable if the subject is composited into a new background. The Extract filter enables you to select detailed edges by painting over them with a brush – you can preview the selection, and modify it

This hairy hound's intricate edges would be impossible to select with the Magnetic Lasso Tool, but the Extract filter is up to the task

if necessary using other brush-based tools, giving you a high degree of control over the selection process.

THE EXTRACT FILTER INTERFACE

1 *Use the Edge Highlighter Tool (B) to draw a freehand selection around the edges of the object you want to extract. This will create a green border.*

2 *Use the Fill Tool (G) to define the area you want to keep by clicking inside the green border to turn the pixels within it purple.*

4 *In Preview Mode the Cleanup Tool (C) enables you to remove any remaining unwanted pixels. Hold [Alt]/[Option] to use the tool to restore pixels that haven't been selected.*

3 *Press Preview to see how your extracted subject looks. You're unlikely to get it right first time, and you can fine-tune the selection using the Cleanup Tool.*

5 *The Edge Touchup Tool (T) is designed to clean up rough edges, although you're better off sticking with the more effective Cleanup Tool.*

6 *If you select Smart Highlighting the brush size will change as you paint around the outline of the dog, becoming smaller where edges are well-defined.*

Magic Extractor

The Extract filter has been around for years, and a revamped version can be found in Elements 4

Photoshop's Extract filter hasn't been updated in the last few versions of Photoshop. While it's an effective tool it can be slow to use, as you usually have to tidy up the initial selection using the Cleanup Tool to get rid of stray pixels, and restore pixels that haven't been selected. The latest version of Photoshop Elements is always worth a look, as it often contains tools that will end up in the next full version of Photoshop. Elements 4 features a revamped version of the Extract filter called the Magic Extractor, and

The Magic Extractor can do an even better job of selecting the stray hairs around the dog's outline than the Extract filter

this new and improved tool can deal with our hairy hound's outline much more effectively, as you'll see.

Trim that fringe
We looked at ways to remove unwanted colour fringes on page 69, and the Magic Extractor has its own fringe-removal tool to help you fine-tune selections. In the Touch Up section of the interface go to Defringe Width, and type in a pixel value – 2 or 3 should be adequate. Click Defringe, and any unwanted pixels clinging to your subject's outline will be removed.

USING MAGIC EXTRACTOR

A few scribbles are enough to isolate objects with complex edges

The Magic Extractor is easier to use than the Extract filter, as you don't have to draw an outline around the object you want to keep. Go to Image > Magic Extractor. Select the Foreground Brush Tool (B), and scribble on the dog's body in red – be careful not to stray into the background. Next select the Background Brush Tool (P) and scribble on the background in blue. Click Preview. The Magic Extractor takes longer to calculate the extraction than the Extract filter, but it's worth the wait. The background will be removed, leaving the dog and its finely detailed hairs intact. Erase any stray background pixels with the Remove From Selection Tool (D).

It may take a while to calculate the extraction, but the Magic Extractor does an impressive job

The Pen Tool

The Pen Tool is perfect for quickly selecting objects that feature lots of curved lines

Perfect paths
The Pen Tool does a great job of selecting curved and straight lines with the minimum of anchor points. An added advantage of the tool is that you can save your paths, so that you can call them up and edit them at any time, even after you've closed and reopened a file. This gives it the edge over tools such as the Magnetic Lasso, which only create temporary selections. Note that Elements doesn't feature the Pen Tool.

We've seen how different selection tools are designed for different jobs, and the Pen Tool (P) comes into its own if you want to select an object that's made up of straight lines and smooth curves, such as a car, or, as you'll see on the next couple of pages, a sailing boat. Like the Magnetic Lasso Tool, the Pen Tool places anchor points to trace the outline of a subject, and by dragging the mouse as you click you can curve the line, or path, in any direction, enabling you to select large curved areas more quickly than

The Pen Tool can draw straight or curved paths, and you can use a selection of related tools to edit the paths for greater precision

you could using other selection tools. You can use a variety of other tools to modify your selection.

USING THE PEN TOOL

To edit an existing path you can use the Path Selection Tool and the Direct Selection Tool.

The Pen Tool lives in this section of the toolbox. Click and hold to see and select the related tools.

Click to place anchor points and create a path. When you've completed a path it can be edited to create a more precise selection.

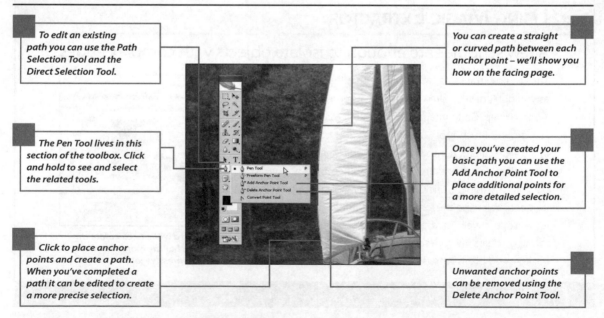

You can create a straight or curved path between each anchor point – we'll show you how on the facing page.

Once you've created your basic path you can use the Add Anchor Point Tool to place additional points for a more detailed selection.

Unwanted anchor points can be removed using the Delete Anchor Point Tool.

Creating a path

Put the Pen Tool through its paces to isolate a boat's curved sails from a busy background

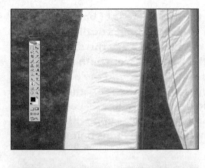

1 Open PenTool.jpg. Select the Pen Tool (P), and make sure Paths is selected in the options bar. Click to place your first anchor point, then, as you click to place the second point, hold down the mouse button and drag. The line will be curved depending on how far, and in which direction, you drag. It can take a while to get the hang of this technique, so you'll need to keep practising.

Paths not shapes
As we mentioned in step 1, before you start making your Pen Tool selection you need to make sure that the tool is set to draw a path – by default the tool is set to create a filled vector shape. You'll see three buttons at the left of the options bar: make sure that the Paths button (the middle one) is selected, rather than 'Shape layer' (the default setting) or 'Fill pixels'.

2 Continue placing points around the sail's outline. Don't worry about being too precise, as you can fine-tune the path later by adding new points and moving existing ones. As you get more experienced with the Pen Tool you'll be able to make selections using a small number of anchor points, enabling you to make smoother selections quickly.

3 Keep clicking to select the outline of the boat – don't worry about areas enclosed by the sail, as you'll add these to the selection later. You'll need to place a few more anchor points around the person's head to add them to the path.

PenTool.mov
To see the Pen Tool being used to select the boat in real time check out this video tutorial on the CD. You'll see how quick and easy it is to select a curved object against a busy background, and learn how to modify the selection.

4 Complete the outline path by placing the last anchor point on the first – as with the Magnetic Lasso you'll see a small circle appear next to the cursor as you hover over the first point, indicating that the next click will close the path. Once you've completed the path the anchor points will vanish. Open the Paths palette to see a preview of your path in white.

Creating a path continued

You can fine-tune your basic path by editing the points and placing additional ones

Points and paths
Sometimes the Direct Selection Tool will move the entire path, instead of individual anchor points, and this can be annoying. If the anchor points are ready to be edited they will appear as square outlines. If the entire path is going to be edited then the anchor points will appear as solid squares; click outside the path, then reselect it and you should now be able to edit points individually.

Editing curves
When you drag an anchor point's Bezier curve handle it tends to curve the path lines on both sides of the anchor point. If you only want to adjust the curve on one side of the point click the curve handle to select it, then hold down the [Alt]/[Option] key. This enables you to tweak the curve on one side of the point without affecting the curve on the other side.

5 Now to remove areas of background from within the boat's outline. With the Pen Tool still selected go to the options bar and click the 'Subtract from path area (-)' button. Draw a path around the area of background between the sails, and the areas enclosed by the railings – you'll see corresponding grey holes appear in the path's thumbnail in the Paths palette.

6 Before you turn the path into a selection you need to fine-tune it. Zoom in to take a closer look at the path – you're likely to find that some lines don't follow the outline of the boat precisely. To adjust the position of an anchor point go to the Path Selection Tool's toolbox compartment, and click and hold to select the Direct Selection Tool (or press A twice).

7 Click on a path line to activate it. You can now manually reposition anchor points by clicking and dragging them to change the length and direction of the lines, and you can also drag a point's Bezier curve handles to alter the shape of curved lines.

8 If you're having trouble selecting some areas accurately you can use the Add Anchor Point Tool to place additional points. Simply move the tool over the path and a + sign will appear beside the icon. Click to add an anchor point (hold down the mouse button and drag if you want to create a curve), and edit the point as above using the Direct Selection Tool.

From path to selection

Once you're happy with your path you can turn it into a conventional selection marquee

1 **Before turning a path into a selection** It's good practice to save it for future use. To turn your temporary 'work path' into a permanently stored path open the Paths palette menu by clicking the arrow button at the top-right of the palette – select Save Path and give the path a name. The path will be stored with the image, and you'll be able to reactivate it and edit it at any time.

Sea.jpg
You'll find this much more photogenic background for our boat on the CD. You can blend the base of the boat with the sea more effectively by using the Eraser Tool (E). Set the tool's opacity to around 30%, and apply it to the base of the boat to fade the pixels slightly.

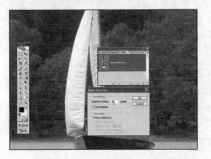

2 **To turn the path into a selection** return to the palette menu and choose Make Selection. The Make Selection dialog appears, enabling you to feather the edge of the selection: a value of 1 pixel should do. Make sure that Anti-aliased is ticked as well, so that the selection's curves and diagonals don't look too jagged. Click OK to create the selection with a 'marching ants' border.

3 **Access the Layers palette by clicking** its tab. The Background layer will be locked, so double-click it to unlock it and make the layer editable. Go to Select > Inverse, or press [Ctrl]/[Command]+[Shift]+I, to select the background instead of the boat, and hit [Backspace]. The background will be deleted, leaving a chequerboard pattern that represents transparency.

Masked alternative
Instead of deleting the boat's background in step 11 you could use a layer mask to hide it instead. Once you've activated the 'marching ants' don't invert the selection; click the 'Add layer mask' button at the foot of the Layers palette instead, and the unselected background will vanish. This will enable you to modify your selection at any time, as the background pixels will still be accessible. We'll take a closer look at creating and modifying layer masks on pages 80-81.

4 **Press [Ctrl]/[Command]+D to deselect** the boat. You can now place a new image behind the boat – perhaps, as here, to display it in more exotic surroundings (see sidebar). The feathering around the edges of the selection will help to blend the boat's pixels with the new background, creating a more convincing composite.

Quick Mask mode

You can fine-tune a selection created with any tool by simply painting on it with brushes

Quick switch

To quickly switch the foreground colour between black and white when you're editing a selection hit X. You can also jump between Quick Mask mode and standard editing mode by pressing Q, to see how your edited selection is shaping up. If you double-click the Quick Mask button the Quick Mask Options dialog appears – you can change the mask colour, and specify whether the colour indicates masked or selected areas.

You've been introduced to many powerful selection tools in this chapter, but you'll find that no tool makes a perfect selection every time – sometimes the tool will have missed part of a background that you need to delete, and other times it'll have selected pixels that you want to keep. You can fine-tune your selections by editing them in Quick Mask mode. On page 69 you had to reduce the Magic Wand's Tolerance setting to stop it selecting pixels in the building as well as in the sky. Quick Mask mode enables

Here areas of brickwork have been selected, as well as the unwanted sky. You can use Quick Mask mode to modify the selection

you to use the default Tolerance setting, and remove the selected areas of the building afterwards.

EDITING A MASK

Switch between black and white brushes to adjust a selection

Press Q to switch to Quick Mask mode, or click the right-hand button below the colour swatches in the toolbox. Unselected areas of the image will turn red, making it easy to spot the areas that have been selected by the Magic Wand, as they'll remain their original colour. Press B to activate the Brush Tool, press D to make sure the foreground colour is the default black, and paint over the areas you want to remove from the selection – they'll turn red as you do so. To add pixels to a selection set the foreground color to white – when you paint over red areas they'll become visible, to indicate that they're part of the selection.

Paint on the mask with a white or black brush to add pixels to, or remove pixels from a selection

The Selection Brush Tool

You can also edit selections with brushes in Elements 4, by using the Selection Brush Tool

1 Open Sign2.jpg from the CD. Select the Magic Wand, and untick Contiguous so you that can select every white sky pixel in one click, including areas among the leaves. The selection is far from perfect. As well as the sky, lettering on the signpost has been selected. It's also hard for the Magic Wand to distinguish between the sky and the edges of the soft-focus leaf in the foreground.

Magic Selection Brush
The Selection Brush Tool shares a compartment with the Magic Selection Brush, which is very similar to Photoshop's Magic Wand. To use it simply scribble on the object that you want to select, and Elements will do its best to isolate the object from its background. The Magic Selection Brush works well when you're selecting well-defined objects against a plain background, but it's less effective for more complex selection tasks.

2 To fine-tune the selection choose the Selection Brush Tool (A); it shares a compartment with the Magic Selection Brush. In the options bar click the 'Subtract from selection' button, and select Mask from the Mode menu. Unselected pixels will appear as red, just as they do in Photoshop's Quick Mask mode.

3 Paint over the lettering's white highlights to turn them red and remove them from the selection. To improve the selection around the leaf go to the options bar and change Hardness to 35% to create a soft-edged selection. Click the 'Add to selection' button, and paint around the edge of the leaf to remove some of the red border, and add more white sky to the selection.

Brush tip tip
When you're using the Selection Brush, or editing a mask with brushes, you'll need to keep adjusting the size of the brush tip to work on areas of differing detail. A quick way to do this is to use the square bracket keys. The left square bracket key ([) shrinks the brush tip, and the right square bracket key (]) enlarges it.

4 You can also edit the marquee without using the red mask. Change Mode to Selection to make the mask disappear. Now, as you paint with the Selection Brush Tool, you'll see the 'marching ants' border change. The fact that you can see your brush strokes modifying the marquee in real time gives the Selection Brush Tool the edge over Photoshop's Quick Mask mode.

Layer masks

Photoshop's layer mask feature enables you to modify your selections whenever you want

Layer masks vs Quick Mask mode
Layer masks enable you to edit a selection marquee created using any of Photoshop's selection tools. Like Quick Mask mode, layer masks enable you to modify the selection using brushes. The key difference is that layer masks can be accessed at any time, as they're permanently stored in the Layers palette, while masks created in Quick Mask mode are temporary.

Most selection tools create a temporary marquee, and you can then copy or otherwise modify selected pixels. Once the 'marching ants' border has been deselected it has gone for good, and any pixels that you've selected and deleted are permanently erased too. One way of giving yourself more flexibility when you're making selections is to use layer masks. The beauty of layer masks is that they can be used to hide selected pixels without permanently erasing them, so you can hide or reveal pixels at any time,

This post box is a tough selection challenge. It contains several different shades of red, some of which are also present in the background car

and fine-tune selections at your leisure. You can also create a selection based on the edited mask.

AN IMPERFECT SELECTION

Our initial Color Range selection is going to need some tidying up

Open the file LetterBox.jpg, and use the Color Range dialog to select the post box (see pages 70–71 for more on the Color Range command). Parts of the post box will be hard to select as they're in shadow, and you'll also find it hard to select all its red tones without selecting the red car in the background. Ideally, the entire post box should turn white to indicate that it has been selected, while the background should be completely black, and unselected. This is virtually impossible to do using only the Color Range dialog, but in the walkthrough opposite we'll show you how to make an imperfect selection perfect using the power of layer masks.

Not all of the reds in the post box have been selected, while parts of the car in the background have

Layer masks in action

Here's how to tweak the initial selection to perfection using a layer mask and brushes

1 After making the selection using the Color Range dialog you'll see some 'marching ants' marching around where they shouldn't be. There are lots of holes in the selection within the outline of the post box, and unwanted parts of the car in the background have been selected as well. Double-click the Background layer thumbnail to unlock it and make it editable.

Hide and seek
It's helpful to be able to see the hidden areas of the masked layer so that you can see how your editing is going. If you click the mask while holding down the [Shift] key you can disable it – a red cross will appear over the mask's thumbnail. To reactivate the mask [Shift]-click on it again. If you [Alt]/[Option]-click on the mask it'll appear in the main work area, which will help you to spot small areas that you might have missed.

2 Click the 'Add a mask' button at the foot of the Layers palette to turn the marquee selection into a greyscale layer mask. The white parts of the mask make the layer's corresponding pixels 100% solid, and black parts of the mask make pixels 100% transparent. Any grey areas on the mask will make the corresponding pixels semi-transparent to varying degrees.

3 Press D to reset the foreground and background colours to black and white if necessary, then hit X to change the foreground colour to white. Select the Brush Tool (B), and click the layer mask to target it. Paint with the white brush over the areas you want to add to the selection, changing the brush tip's size as you work using the square bracket keys.

Masks In Elements
Photoshop Elements doesn't enable you to create layer masks in the same way Photoshop does. However, if you make a selection and then create an adjustment layer you'll notice that the adjustment layer does contain a layer mask, and you can modify this mask using black and white brushes as shown here.

4 Press X to change the foreground colour to black. Now you can paint out unwanted background pixels until only the post box remains. Switch between a white and black brush to modify the mask until it's perfect. When you've finished editing the mask hold down [Ctrl]/[Command] and click on the layer mask's thumbnail to load it as a selection.

Creative masking

You can also use layer masks to hide or reveal all kinds of image adjustments and effects

Zoom blur
You can add motion blur to a static object when you photograph it. By setting the camera to a slow shutter speed, and manually zooming out as you capture the image, you can create a dramatic zoom blur effect. It's tricky to do, however, and you can easily end up overexposing the image. By adding the blur in Photoshop you have much more control over the effect.

On the previous page we showed you how to tidy up a selection by using black and white brushes to hide and reveal pixels on a layer mask. You can also paint on a mask using different shades of grey, which enables you to turn pixels on the main layer semi-transparent, instead of hiding them or revealing them entirely. The ability of layer masks to hide or reveal pixels to varying degrees makes them ideal for fine-tuning creative edits such as filter effects, and on the facing page we'll show you how you can

This sharp shot of a vehicle can be made more interesting by adding a touch of motion blur, and then editing the effect with a mask

use black, white and grey brushes on a mask to enhance a photo by fine-tuning a blurring effect.

MOTION BLUR

Go from 0 to 60 in seconds with the help of the Motion Blur filter

Motion blur is a great way of adding a sense of speed and drama to a shot of a vehicle. You could attempt to capture real motion blur by setting your camera to a slow shutter speed, and shooting a bike or car driving by, but getting the shot right is a tricky job – you can easily end up with the vehicle looking too blurred, and if you mistime the shot part of the vehicle might even have left the frame. By adding motion blur in Photoshop you can compose the image exactly as you want. You can then use the layer mask technique to reduce the amount of blurring in selected areas, so that you can see details such as faces.

A blur filter can obscure important detail – a layer mask will help you to create a more selective blur effect

Selective motion blur

Use layer masks to edit a blur effect so that you can preserve detail in particular areas

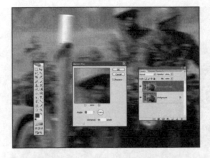

1 Open MotionBlur.jpg from the CD. Duplicate the Background layer by dragging it on to the 'Create a new layer' button at the foot of the Layers palette, and target the new layer by clicking its thumbnail. Go to Filter > Blur > Motion Blur. Choose an Angle of -5 to make the blur match the direction the motorcycle is moving in, and set Distance to 58 pixels.

2 Click OK to apply the Motion Blur filter to the duplicated layer. At this stage the entire image will become blurred, including objects that should be static, such as the foreground post. Click the 'Add a mask' button in the Layers palette. A white mask icon will appear next to the blurred layer's thumbnail.

3 Press D to reset the default toolbox colours. Press B to select the Brush Tool, then open the Brush Preset picker and choose a fairly large soft-edged brush. Click the mask's thumbnail to target it, and paint over the wooden post in the image. The blurred pixels will become 100% transparent, revealing the unblurred post on the Background layer.

4 Click the foreground colour swatch in the toolbox to open the Color Picker, and select a grey. Click OK. When you paint grey on the mask you turn the layer's pixels semi-transparent. This is an effective way of restoring partial detail to the figures, and parts of the bike such as the number plate, while preserving the stronger blur around the edges of the vehicle.

Blurring in Elements
You can't add a layer mask to your blur layer in Elements 4. However, you can reduce the amount of blurring with the Eraser Tool. Set the tool's opacity to 100% to completely remove the blur from areas, and reduce the opacity to mimic the effect of using a grey brush on a layer mask, and make pixels semi-transparent.

Hide all
To add a white 'reveal all' mask to a layer you could also go to Layer > Add Layer Mask > Reveal All. If you select Hide All instead, or hold down [Alt]/[Option] as you press the 'Add a mask' button, the mask will hide the adjustment or filter effect. The mask thumbnail will be black, rather than white, and you can paint the effect back in as necessary with a white brush.

Faking reflections

Create a perfectly symmetrical reflection by transforming and editing a selection

Reflection.jpg
Follow the walkthrough on the facing page to select the rippling water in our source image and replace it with a perfect reflection.

There are many reasons for making a selection. You might simply want to change the colour of an object, or remove a boring sky and replace it with a more colourful and interesting one. In earlier chapters we demonstrated how the camera's aperture and shutter speed settings can easily spoil a shot, and external factors such as the weather can also foil our efforts to capture the perfect picture. A gust of wind is all it takes to distort the surface of a lake and ruin a reflection, but by creating and modifying selections

The wind-rippled water breaks up the reflection of the surrounding landscape in this shot, but we can fake the perfect image in Photoshop

we can easily create the effect of the landscape being reflected in a mirror-smooth body of water.

SELECT, TRANSFORM AND BLUR

We'll use a whole range of tools to create our reflection effect

Thanks to Photoshop you can create the perfect reflection shot without having to wait for the weather to improve – and in Britain that could be a long wait! In the walkthrough on the facing page we'll show you how to isolate the water in our source image, and replace the rippled surface with a mirror image of the landscape. After using the Magnetic Lasso to select the water we'll replace it with a Rectangular Marquee selection of the landscape, and use the Edit > Transform menu to flip this selection to create the reflection. To complete the effect we'll use the Radial Blur filter to add some texture to the surface of our 'lake'.

On the facing page we'll show you how to replace the distorted reflection with this perfectly smooth one

Creating a reflection effect

Here's how to replace a distorted reflection with something altogether more striking

1 Open the file Reflection.jpg from the CD. Select the Rectangular Marquee Tool (M), and in the options bar set Feather to 2 pixels to create a soft-edged selection. Draw a selection marquee that includes the mountains and the trees by the shoreline, and Edit > Copy the selection (or hit [Ctrl]/[Command]+C) to save the selected pixels to Photoshop's clipboard.

2 As the lake is irregular in shape select the Magnetic Lasso Tool (L) so that you can quickly trace its edges. Set the tool's Feather option to 6 pixels; this will make it easier to blend the edges of the fake reflection with the surrounding pixels in the next step. Go to Edit > Paste Into to paste the copied background into the lake selection as a new layer.

3 The 'marching ants' border around the lake will vanish. A layer mask based on the lake selection will be applied to the new layer, and the pasted background will only be visible within the confines of the selection. To turn the pasted landscape into a reflection go to Edit > Transform > Flip Vertical. Use the Move Tool (V) to position the reflection as shown.

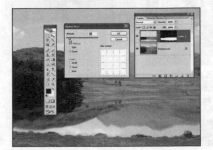

4 The flipped reflection is a little too clean and clinical. Give it a sense of depth and perspective by targeting the reflection layer and going to Filter > Render > Radial Blur. Set Amount to 10, Blur Method to Zoom and Quality to Good, and click OK. This roughs-up the surface of the 'lake' a little, while still preserving enough detail to create a convincing reflection.

Edge Contrast
When you're selecting the lake's surface in step 2 the Magnetic Lasso Tool might have trouble telling the difference between the dark edges of the lake and the shoreline. Give it a helping hand by changing the Edge Contrast setting to 7% – this will make the tool more sensitive to subtle differences in contrast.

Brushing up
You can fine-tune the edges of the fake reflection layer by painting with a black or white brush on the layer mask – this will enable you to improve on the Magnetic Lasso selection. For more information on modifying selections using layer masks refer back to pages 80–81.

Selective focus

Another use for layer masks is to fake a 'depth of field' effect to highlight subjects in a photo

Depth of field
When your camera's aperture is open as wide as it can go you'll find that it creates a very shallow depth of field. This means it's hard to get objects that are at different distances from the lens in focus, especially if some of those objects are near the camera. A smaller aperture setting of around f/10 creates a wider depth of field, making it easier to get everything in focus. You can then selectively blur areas using Photoshop.

By now you should be well up to speed on the concept of layer masks. These wonderfully versatile tools enable you to fine-tune selections to perfection, or restrict an image adjustment or filter effect to particular parts of an image. A popular use for layer masks is to modify a Gaussian Blur filter effect to alter the focal point of a photograph. In our sample shot (FocalPoint.jpg on the CD) both the main subjects and the background are in focus. You can blur the background to draw attention to the

This shot's sharply focused busy background distracts the eye from the main subjects – we can fix that by blurring the background

foreground subjects by using the layer mask technique described in the box below.

FAKING DEPTH OF FIELD

Blur the background to focus attention on foreground subjects

You could set your aperture to make the camera focus on the happy couple in the foreground, and blur the people in the background (see sidebar). But during a hectic wedding shoot there's not always time to play around with aperture settings. To adjust the focus in Photoshop open FocalPoint. jpg. Duplicate the Background layer, go to Filter > Blur > Gaussian Blur and enter a Radius value of 15 (you could also use the more configurable Lens Blur filter if you have it). Add a layer mask to the blurred layer, and paint with a soft-edged black brush on the mask to reveal the bride and groom from the layer below, while keeping the rest of the layer blurred.

Use a black brush on a layer mask to remove the blur effect from areas you want to focus on

Silhouette effect

Modify a selection to create the effect of a subject being backlit by the setting sun

1 Open Swimmer.jpg from the CD. We'll modify a selection to make our subject look like he's emerging from the sea at sunset. Double-click the Background layer to unlock it. Use the Magnetic Lasso or Pen Tool to draw around the figure's outline, and fine-tune the selection as necessary. Go to Select > Inverse ([Ctrl]/[Command]+[Shift]+I) to select the background, and delete it.

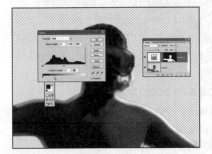

2 Use the Magic Wand Tool to select the transparent background around the figure. Go to Select > Modify > Expand, and enter a value of around 50 pixels. This will tighten the selection marquee so that it cuts into the figure, but still follows his outline. Right-click ([Ctrl]-click) inside the selection and choose Feather, and in the dialog enter 10 to create a soft-edged selection. Click OK.

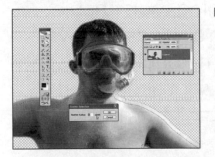

3 Go to Select > Inverse again to select the swimmer. Add a Levels adjustment layer, and drag the white point Output Levels slider to the left, to around 72. This will darken the body of the figure, but leave a halo of light around his edges, as if he's being backlit by the setting sun. Click OK.

4 To complete the illusion of our figure emerging from the sea at sunset open Silhouette.jpg. Choose Select > All, copy the image, and paste it into the swimmer file as a new layer. Place the layer below the swimmer layer in the Layers palette. The Levels adjustment layer won't affect this new background layer, as the layer mask limits the adjustment to the figure.

Warm light
The light around the edge of the swimmer is not as warm as the glow of the setting sun. To warm it up right-click ([Ctrl]-click) on the swimmer's thumbnail and choose Select Layer Transparency. The 'marching ants' will appear. Add a Color Balance adjustment layer – you can then increase the strength of the red and yellow pixels in the image to warm up the light on the swimmer.

Spoiled for choice
In this chapter we've looked at many different tools and techniques for making and modifying selections, and you should be able to adapt these techniques, and configure the tools as necessary, to tackle any selection challenges you encounter with your own images.

MASTER THE CLONING AND HEALING TOOLS

Photoshop's powerful cloning tools enable you to alter your images in all kinds of ways, from quickly covering up minor blemishes to removing a person from a shot altogether!

They say the camera never lies, but even in the pre-digital days photographers were able to use a variety of techniques to make their cameras bend the truth a little. For example, a filters placed over the lens, combined with a strong light source, made it possible to create wrinkle-free portrait shots that flattered their subjects by taking years off them. Photographers could also touch-up their prints in the darkroom in order to remove unsightly spots and blemishes. With the advent of digital photography and powerful image-editing software such as Photoshop, it's easier than ever to use your computer to manipulate any photo that you've taken and create a subtly altered version of the truth. You could even turn reality completely on its head.

Digital deception

At the subtle end of the image editing scale the healing and cloning tools in Photoshop and Elements enable you to tidy up your images by removing blemishes from a subject's face or by erasing any distracting background objects from a landscape shot. Some people might argue that editing images in this way is somehow dishonest, but these kinds of minor alterations can hardly be described as image manipulation,

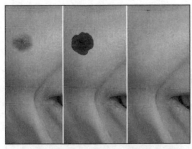

Page 90 *Banish blemishes with the gentle touch of the Spot Healing Brush*

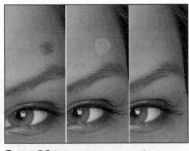

Page 90 *Take greater control over your editing with the Healing Brush*

Page 91 *Remove large unwanted objects in seconds using the Patch Tool*

Page 92 *Use the Clone Stamp Tool to replace elements with surrounding pixels*

Page 93 *Transform a Polygonal Lasso selection to cover up unwanted objects*

Page 94 *Use CS2's Vanishing Point filter to clone and heal in perspective*

any more than altering the contrast or colour of a shot can. All you're really doing is creating an image that shows off your subject in the best possible way.

Crossing the line

At the other end of the scale you can transform an image dramatically so that it bears little resemblance to the original. For example, you could remove a person from an image entirely. It's a matter of opinion as to where you draw the line between edits that enhance a shot, and edits that create a fake version of reality. However, we're not here to discuss the ethics of image manipulation;

but wherever that line happens to be, we'll show you how you can cross it!

In this chapter you'll discover how easy it is to remove unwanted objects using the Healing Brush and Spot Healing Brush tools, and we'll show you how to take pixels from one part of an image and transplant them elsewhere using the Clone Stamp Tool. You'll also discover how to transform pixels and use them as patches, a technique you can take even further using CS2's powerful Vanishing Point filter. Once we've shown you how to use the tools it's up to you what you do with them, and to decide exactly how truthful you want your images to be!

The healing tools

For small touch-up jobs use the Healing Brush Tool, or the Spot Healing Brush if you have it

Spot Healing options
By default the Spot Healing Brush is set to Proximity Match in the options bar, and will sample pixels close to the spot or blemish. This is fine if you're working on skin, as it creates a smooth and seamless repair. If you're working on a more textured surface, such as grass, then you don't want the patch to be smooth, so choose the Create Texture option to create a repair that incorporates the texture of the surrounding pixels.

Photoshop's healing and cloning tools are closely related, and they do a similar job of sampling pixels from one part of an image and transplanting them to cover problem areas. If you have Photoshop CS2, or Elements 3 or 4, then to remove minor blemishes such as a spot on the skin you can try the Spot Healing Brush Tool (J). Simply click and drag to paint over the offending spot; when you release the mouse button the pixels that you've defined will be altered to take on the colour and tone of the surrounding pixels, and

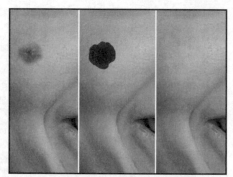

You can banish minor blemishes like this one in an instant with a quick spray of the Spot Healing Brush Tool

the healed area will also be blended with the neighbouring pixels to create a seamless repair.

THE HEALING BRUSH TOOL

Use this tool to choose which pixels are used to cover up a spot

The Spot Healing Brush is great for removing spots that are surrounded by similarly coloured and textured pixels, such as a mole on smooth skin. If the spot is near the subject's hair, however, there's a danger that the tool will incorporate hair pixels in the repair. The Healing Brush Tool (J) enables you to choose which pixels are sampled to replace the blemish. Hold down [Alt]/[Option] to sample a patch of clean skin, then spray over the spot; as with the Spot Healing Brush, the repaired area will be blended with surrounding pixels. The healing tools aren't just for skin – they're perfect for jobs such as removing a scratch from a car's paintwork.

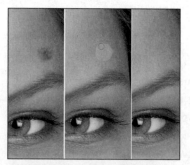

Use the Healing Brush to sample a clear patch of skin if the spot is close to an area of differing colour

The Patch Tool

If the healing tools struggle to remove larger objects from an image, reach for the Patch Tool

The Healing Brush and Spot Healing Brush are great for quickly erasing small blemishes, but they have their limitations. Open Patch.jpg, and try using the Spot Healing Brush (if you have it) to remove the dog. With the Proximity Match option selected you'll replace the dog with an unconvincing blob of smooth green pixels, and even with Create Texture selected the patch will still be noticeable. You won't fair much better with the Healing Brush – the dog is too large in the frame, and the background

Neither the Healing Brush nor the Spot Healing Brush will remove the dog from this image effectively, but the Patch Tool will

grass is too detailed, for either tool to remove it effectively. This is a job for Photoshop's Patch Tool (J).

Patch.mov
To see how quick and effective the Patch Tool can be check out this video tutorial on the CD. We'll also demonstrate the difference between the healing tools and the Patch Tool, to give you a better idea of when to use which one.

USING THE PATCH TOOL

Remove unwanted objects in seconds by dragging a selection

Select the Patch Tool – its location in the toolbox depends on which version of Photoshop you're using. Select Source in the options bar, and draw around the dog, making sure to include its shadow, to create a selection marquee. Drag this selection to an area of clear grass, and you'll see that these pixels appear in place of the dog in the patch. Release the mouse button, and press [Ctrl]/[Command]+D to deselect the marquee; as with the healing tools, the patch will be blended with the surrounding pixels. Alternatively, you can select Destination in the options bar, then select an area of clear grass and drag this over the dog.

Remove large areas of unwanted pixels in seconds, and create a seamless repair, with the Patch Tool

The Clone Stamp Tool

Remove detailed objects from images by replacing them with surrounding pixels

Clone.mov
In this video tutorial we'll show you how easy it is to use the Clone Stamp Tool to remove an unwanted figure that overlaps a busy background. You'll also find out how to avoid some of the pitfalls novice cloners can fall into, such as accidentally sampling and cloning parts of the figure that you want to erase.

Brush options
The Clone Stamp Tool uses a brush, and this can be configured in the same way as any Photoshop brush. You can increase the softness of the brush tip to make your cloned areas blend more effectively with their surroundings, and clone larger areas by increasing the diameter of the brush tip.

1 Open Clone.jpg. We're going to remove the girl from the scene to give the shot a better balance. Select the Clone Stamp Tool, and click the 'Create a new layer' button in the Layers palette – cloning pixels on to a new layer gives you more control over the process. In the options bar tick Aligned, and tick Sample All layers so that you can sample pixels from the Background layer.

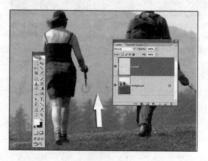

2 Hold down [Alt]/[Option], and click to sample the area where the grass meets the trees, just to the right of the girl. Now move the cursor to the left until it rests over the base of her walking stick. Click to spray the sampled pixels over the walking stick; as you move upwards you'll spray sampled trees and parts of the background mountain over the stick.

3 Take a new sample, and start cloning-out the girl's feet. As the crosshairs remain aligned with the sampled pixels you can spray the tops of trees from a clear part of the image on to the trees that were obscured by the figure. Sample new areas often – this helps you to avoid creating repetitive patterns that will give away the fact that the image has been manipulated.

4 Once you've replaced the girl's legs with the grass and trees you can start sampling and cloning bits of mountain from her left side. As the mountain is fairly indistinct it's easier to sample random pixels and replace the top part of the figure.

Patching in perspective

Photos shot at an angle pose a challenge for the Clone Stamp and Healing Brush tools

On the previous page we were able to clone-out the girl very effectively by sampling areas of scenery that were similar to those she was obscuring. However, the Clone Stamp Tool will have a tougher time of it if you're working on photos that have been taken from an angle. You can't clone pixels from a distant object and use them to replace a foreground object, because the scale of the transplanted pixels will be wrong. CS2 users have a tool that enables them to clone pixels in perspective, which we'll look at over

It would be difficult, and very time-consuming, to replace the foreground windows and sign with background pixels using the Clone Stamp

the page, but before we do so here's a technique that pre-CS2 and Elements users can employ.

Soft option
When you create the patch with the Polygonal Lasso Tool, set Feather to 2 pixels in the options bar to give your copied pixels a soft edge. This will help the patch to merge more effectively with the pixels on the layer below. A non-feathered patch would be more noticeable.

TRANSFORMING SELECTIONS

Copy, move and then transform a suitable patch of pixels

To replace the dummy foreground windows with real ones, and remove the sign, start by selecting the Polygonal Lasso. Place four corner points to select the two middle windows and the wall below them, following the perspective of the building along the horizontal lines. Copy the selection, paste it, and use the Move Tool to place it over the foreground windows. Go to Edit > Transform > Scale. Hold down [Shift] to constrain the proportions of the patch, and drag the top-left and bottom-right corner handles to extend the patch over the foreground windows. Fine-tune the fit using the corner handles, and other Transform options if necessary.

The Transform > Scale option enables you to adjust the patch to match the perspective of the building

Vanishing Point

Copy, paste and clone selections in perfect perspective with this amazing CS2 feature

Marquee Tool
Once you've defined a plane you can clone pixels and watch them scale up or down as you move them around the image, and you can also use the Rectangular Marquee Tool to create selections that match the perspective of the image. Once you've made a marquee selection hold down [Alt]/[Option] and drag it to a new position, and it will be scaled up or down accordingly.

Vanish.mov
If you don't have CS2 you can see Vanishing Point being put through its paces by watching our video tutorial on the CD. It may even inspire you to upgrade!

1 The select and transform technique demonstrated on the previous page used to be the only solution for images that contained perspective. CS2's Vanishing Point filter enables you to define an image's perspective plane, and cloned or copied pixels will be scaled up or down accordingly. Open Vanishing.jpg and go to Filter > Vanishing Point.

2 The Vanishing Point interface will open. To define the perspective plane select the Create Plane Tool (C) from the mini-toolbox. Click four times to draw a polygon that encompasses the two false windows, and the two real windows next to them. The grid that represents the plane will turn blue.

3 The plane is accurately following the perspective of the four windows, but it's too small to include other details, such as the sign and the brickwork below the windows. Select the Edit Plane Tool (V), and drag the white handles at the edges of the plane outwards so that it expands to cover the top section of the building.

4 Select the Stamp Tool – it's Vanishing Point's version of the Clone Stamp. Press [Alt]/[Option] to sample the bottom-right corner of the first complete window, and move the cursor to the equivalent point on the fake foreground window – you'll see a floating preview of the scaled-up sampled pixels, which enables you to accurately place them over the area you want to cover.

Vanishing Point

Clone-out the foreground windows and sign using the sampled background window

5 Use the Diameter option to reduce the brush size, and click to spray the sampled background window's pixels over the foreground window. Keep the mouse button pressed, and try and replace as much of the foreground window as you can in one long spray to create a smooth edit. Keep spraying until the window has been replaced by the sampled pixels.

6 Once you've dealt with the first window release the mouse button, and click to take a new sample from the top-right corner of the window you sampled initially. Place the cursor over the top-right corner of the second false window, then click and spray until the window and sign have been completely replaced.

Paint in perspective
Vanishing Point also has a Brush Tool (B), which enables you to paint in perspective. You can use the Eyedropper Tool to sample a colour from the image, and then paint on the photo using the brush – the brush tip will automatically be scaled down as you paint over distant areas, and scaled up as you paint in the foreground. You could add convincing graffiti to a photo of a wall using this technique.

Healing option
Vanishing Point's Stamp Tool can be configured to behave like the Healing Brush Tool. With the tool selected, go to the options bar and set the Heal option to On. This will cause the edges of transplanted pixels to blend more effectively with their surroundings.

Creative cloning

Use Photoshop's tools to turn a holiday snap into a dramatic digital matte painting

Bridge.jpg
*You'll find our source image Bridge.jpg on the CD. If you don't have CS2 you'll have to resort to using the select and transform technique featured on page 93 to extend the bridge. Once you've done that you can use the Clone Stamp Tool to create a deeper ravine, as shown on page 99. If you want to try out Vanishing Point you can download a trial version of CS2 from **www.adobe.com/ products/photoshop**.*

So far in this chapter we've looked at several ways in which you can harness the pixel-pushing powers of tools such as the Clone Stamp and Vanishing Point to hide unwanted elements, but you can go a great deal further with Photoshop's cloning and transformation tools, and alter the reality of your images in more creative and dramatic ways. In the following walkthrough we'll reveal some more Vanishing Point secrets as we turn a simple holiday snap into something far more dramatic, by transforming a short

This short wooden bridge is hardly something that would give Indiana Jones pause for thought – time to unleash Vanishing Point!

bridge that crosses a shallow drop into a longer and more precarious one spanning a deep ravine.

ON LOCATION

Shoot your source images with a Photoshop makeover in mind

The majority of this Focus Guide covers photo fixing, but once you've mastered using Photoshop's tools to correct and touch-up your images you'll be able to use them in more exciting ways, and unleash your creative side in the process! Our shot of a bridge is just an ordinary holiday snap, and you can frame your own photos with the intention of giving them a Photoshop makeover. On the following pages we'll show you how to use the Vanishing Point filter to extend the bridge in perspective. We'll then show you how to turn the shallow gully into a deep ravine with the help of the Clone Stamp Tool.

You can adapt the techniques in our walkthrough to transform any image in a photorealistic way

Defining the plane

Learn more about Vanishing Point's ability to clone in perspective by extending the bridge

1 **Open Bridge.jpg. If you look at the image's histogram you'll see that it's slightly underexposed, and is lacking detail in the highlights range. It's a good idea to brighten the shot to get it looking its best before you begin your creative editing. Go to Image > Adjustments > Levels, and drag the white point Input Levels slider to the left to brighten up the highlights. Click OK.**

2 **Go to Filter > Vanishing Point. Select the Create Plane Tool, and place four corner points to define the perspective of the wooden fence along the nearside of the bridge. If the perspective you've defined is plausible the grid will turn blue (see sidebar).**

3 **Extend the ends of the grid to the left and right by dragging the white handles, and extend the bottom of the grid downwards. This will ensure that the Stamp Tool will be able to interpret the perspective of the bridge, and clone pixels accordingly.**

4 **Click on the middle square handle at the top edge of the grid. Hold down [Ctrl]/[Command], and drag the handle to the left. This creates a new plane at a right angle to the original plane; you'll use this extra plane to extend the pixels of the rear fence. You can extrapolate as many new planes from your original plane as you like using this technique.**

Seeing red
The grid that you create with the Create Plane Tool tells Photoshop about the image's perspective. If Photoshop can't work out the perspective from the plane you define, the grid will turn red or yellow, to warn you that the Stamp Tool won't work effectively. Only a blue grid will do.

Fine-tuning the plane
Once you've created a perspective plane, and extended it, you can make further adjustments to it. Select the Edit Plane Tool, and drag any of the plane's white corner handles until the grid looks like it's accurately overlaying the bridge. If the grid turns red at any point you'll need to adjust the handles until it turns blue again.

Extending the bridge

When you're happy with your perspective plane you can get to work extending the bridge

No escape!
When you're working in the Vanishing Point filter's interface be careful not to hit the [Esc] key. This will close the filter, and you'll lose your carefully constructed perspective planes, as well as any cloning that you've done!

Save it
When you get to step 8 you're ready to embark on a new cloning operation. Go to File > Save As, and give the image a numerical suffix (for example Bridge02. psd). This will enable you to retrieve this version of the image if things go wrong during the next stage.

5 Select the Stamp Tool. The two blue plane grids will change to two blue outlines – this helps you get a better look at the pixels you're cloning and transplanting. Hold down [Alt]/[Option] and click to sample the top of the post to the right of the figure. Move the cursor to a similar point on the most distant post, and click and drag to extend the wooden railings.

6 Click to sample one of the cloned posts, and use it to continue extending the bridge. Finish extending the nearside of the bridge by spraying in a whole post at the far right of the shot. If your cloned post's pixels don't align perfectly with the original fence posts press [Ctrl]/[Command]+Z to undo the last brush stroke. You can then define a new sample point and have another go.

7 Move the cursor on to the top plane, and click to sample the post on the far side of the bridge and just to the right of the figure. To make that side of the fence look broken, and make the bridge look more dangerous, extend the top rail a short distance to the right. Click OK to apply your Vanishing Point edits, and return to the regular Photoshop work area.

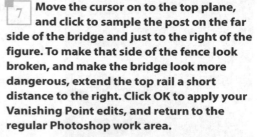

8 Now you're going to create some canvas space to extend the ravine into. Open the Layers palette, and double-click on the Background layer's thumbnail to unlock it. Select the Move Tool (V), and drag the entire layer upwards. You'll see the checkerboard transparency pattern appear below the image.

Dig deeper

Once you've extended the bridge, give it something suitably impressive to span

9 Select the Lasso Tool (L), and draw a selection around the rocks and grass at the base of the bridge. Copy and paste the selection – the copy will appear in the same position on the canvas, but on a new layer. Use the Move Tool (V) to drag the selection down to the bottom of the canvas. Create a new layer, and select the Clone Stamp Tool (S).

New layer
Adding your cloned pixels to a new layer makes it much easier to see what you're doing, and easier to retrace your steps if things go wrong. You can also use the Eraser Tool (E) to delete cloned pixels if necessary, without altering any of the pixels on the other layers.

10 Tick Use All Layers so that the tool can clone from the Background layer and place the cloned pixels on the new transparent layer. Press [Alt]/[Option] to sample areas such as the bracken in the foreground, and fill the transparent areas. Sample rocks and grass from the lower-left of the image, and spray these under the bridge to fill in the gaps.

Non-aligned
If you don't have a large area of suitable pixels to sample untick the Aligned setting in the options bar, then use the Clone Stamp in the normal way. When you release the mouse button, reposition the brush and start spraying again the tool will continue to sample from the original point that you defined, instead of sampling from a new point relative to the brush's position, as is the case when you have the Aligned option ticked.

REMOVING CAMERA ARTIFACTS

As well as failing to capture colour and contrast accurately, your camera can introduce artifacts such as chromatic aberration and lens distortion. In this chapter we'll show you how to fix them

Trying to capture the perfect photograph is a battle from start to finish. In addition to composing the shot correctly, you have to achieve a balance between shutter speed and aperture setting in order to take a correctly exposed shot, and use the correct white balance setting for the prevailing light temperature in order to record accurate colours. It's easy to get these settings wrong, and sometimes your camera will let you down, but fortunately you can depend on Photoshop's tools to get your shots looking their best. We've shown you how to salvage detail in washed-out shadows and clipped highlights, looked at a number of

ways in which you can remove colours casts, and shown you how to remove blemishes and correct composition problems. As well as introducing tone and colour problems there are many other ways in which the camera can sabotage your battle for perfection, and in this chapter we'll show you how to tackle these problems.

Common artifacts

The process of light passing through the lens and on to the camera's sensor can introduce all kinds of shot-spoiling artifacts. A building's vertical lines can look tilted thanks to perspective distortion, so we'll

Page 102 Correct blurring the easy way using the Unsharp Mask filter

Page 103 Use CS2's Smart Sharpen filter to banish blur but preserve detail

Page 105 Use the Transform options to straighten out converging verticals

Page 106 Use an adjustment layer to remove unwanted colour fringes

Page 107 Reduce the effects of noise and JPEG compression artifacts

Page 109 Add artifacts to an image to produce a retro film camera effect

show you how to quickly straighten matters out. Some lenses can cause vignetting, which takes the form of a dark ring around the edges of the frame, while objects that have areas of high contrast (such as the shiny specular highlights on a bike frame) can take on unsightly blue fringes. This latter artifact is called chromatic aberration, and it's such a common problem with digital cameras that Photoshop now contains a dedicated tool for removing it. However, it's not particularly effective so we'll show you a technique for removing colour fringes using any version of Photoshop. We'll also show you the most effective ways to smooth-out picture grain, and pixel-block artifacts that can be introduced by the JPEG compression process.

All of a blur

We might be able to put up with a little chromatic aberration or noise, but a blurred shot will normally be set for a one-way trip to the bin. Blur can be caused by a variety of factors, such as camera movement or incorrect focus settings. Photoshop has a number of sharpening tools, and we'll show you which ones are most effective. By the time you've completed this chapter you'll be ready to deal with any problem your camera can throw at you!

Unsharp Mask

The Unsharp Mask filter is an effective tool for restoring clarity to slightly blurred shots

What's in a name?
Unsharp Mask may seem a strange name for a filter that sharpens things, and this is because it's named after a traditional darkroom tool. Photographers could make their negatives look sharper by adding a blurred mask to them – if you'd like to read about this technique check out Haje Jan Kamp's article at www.photocritic. org/articles/usm.php.

When you view a shot on your camera's LCD screen it often looks sharper than it actually is. Once you see the shot at full size, however, you'll often spot focus-related problems. The shot of our bagpipe player (Pipes.jpg) looks fine when viewed as a thumbnail, but at full size you can see that the image is slightly soft; to see how sharp a shot really is double-click the Zoom Tool in the toolbox to set your image to Actual Pixels view. Fortunately, Photoshop is packed with a variety of sharpening tools, and one of the

The finer details in this shot are blurred due to an incorrect focus setting. We can sharpen them using the Unsharp Mask filter

easiest to use is the Unsharp Mask filter, which you'll find in both Photoshop and Elements.

UNSHARP MASK IN ACTION

Sharpen detail that's been blurred in slightly out-of-focus shots

Open Pipes.jpg from the CD and go to Filter > Sharpen > Unsharp Mask. The filter works by increasing the contrast between pixels to enhance detail. Increase the Amount setting to 152%, and increase the Radius setting slightly. The higher the Radius setting, the more danger there is of burning-out highlights and adding artifacts such as halos around contrasting objects, so try not to increase Radius above 4 pixels. Keep the Threshold slider at 0 so that the subtlest details, such as the hairs on the subject's hand, are sharpened. To compare the sharpened image with the original click and hold on the image preview in the dialog.

We've turned the preview option off so you can see the original image and the sharpened version side by side

Using Smart Sharpen

If you have CS2 you can target sharpening at specific areas to minimise artifacts such as halos

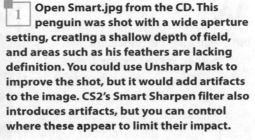

1 **Open Smart.jpg from the CD. This penguin was shot with a wide aperture setting, creating a shallow depth of field, and areas such as his feathers are lacking definition. You could use Unsharp Mask to improve the shot, but it would add artifacts to the image. CS2's Smart Sharpen filter also introduces artifacts, but you can control where these appear to limit their impact.**

2 **Go to Filter > Sharpen > Smart Sharpen. As the penguin is very blurred push the Amount slider to a high 186%. To bring out the fine details in the penguin's feathers you'll need to increase the Radius to 15. Although this gives the feathers more definition it also adds a dark halo where the white feathers contrast with the darker background.**

3 **As the halo is most visible in the darker areas click the Advanced button and open the Shadow tab. You can reduce the sharpening in the shadows while preserving detail in the white feathers. Set Fade Amount to 31%, and increase Tonal Width to 76 so that the sharpening reduction applies to the shadows and midtones. The halo is now less prominent, but the feathers are still sharp.**

4 **Sharpening can cause finer highlight details in the image to become burnt-out, so go to the Highlight tab and set Fade Amount to 4%. This will remove the blown-out highlights from the feathers on the penguin's head, for example.**

Save your sharpening
The Smart Sharpen dialog contains lots of sliders and settings, and you can spend quite a while tinkering with the various options. When you're happy with your image you can save your settings by clicking on the little floppy disc icon. If you need to sharpen a similar image you can load your saved settings from the Settings menu.

Different blurs
The Smart Sharpen filter has the edge over Unsharp Mask because it enables you to target the cause of the blurring more effectively. You can choose the standard Gaussian Blur setting from the Remove menu, or change it to Lens Blur for more effective sharpening. You can even try and remove Motion Blur caused by camera movement, but this particular option tends not to be very effective.

The Lens Correction filter

Correct common lens-induced artifacts with CS2's comprehensive Lens Correction filter

Alignment
When you're correcting an image to get the horizontal lines looking horizontal and the verticals vertical, you need to use the greyscale grid as a guide. For greater accuracy you can use the Lens Correction filter's Move Grid Tool (M) to reposition the lines of the grid, for example to align them with the walls of a building.

W e depend on our camera's lens to capture a good shot, but it can also introduce artifacts that spoil an image. Some lenses can warp an image, causing the edges to curve (barrel distortion), while at their widest setting some lenses add dark patches to the corners of a shot (vignetting). And if you photograph a tall building from close to its base, vertical lines can converge, rather than running parallel with the edge of the frame. CS2 makes correcting these problems easier by placing a selection of lens-related tools in one

This building's converging vertical lines can be straightened out using the Lens Correction filter's Perspective tools

handy interface. We'll introduce you to the tools below, then put the most useful ones through their paces.

Straighten Tool
Elements 4 also has a version of the Straighten Tool. Simply draw a line with the tool along an image's tilted horizon, and the entire image will be rotated so that the line you've drawn runs parallel with the bottom edge of the frame. You'll need to crop the shot to remove the transparent areas that appear.

KEY LENS CORRECTION TOOLS

REMOVE DISTORTION – Drag this slider to the left to correct images suffering from pincushion distortion (where the image bulges inwards), or right to remove barrel distortion (where the image bulges outwards).

CHROMATIC ABERRATION – This slider attempts to remove fringes around contrasting edges, although it's not particularly successful. Check out page 106 for an alternative technique.

VIGNETTE – Use this slider to lighten dark patches in the corners of a shot. You can widen or narrow the area of adjustment using the Midpoint slider.

TRANSFORM – This section of the interface enables you to adjust a shot's horizontal or vertical perspective to combat perspective distortion. You can also rotate a shot to straighten tilted horizons using the Angle control.

STRAIGHTEN TOOL – This clever tool enables you to straighten tilted horizons in an instant – see the sidebar for more information.

Perspective distortion

Correct perspective distortion the 'old' way, then try out the Lens Correction filter's tools

C S2's Lens Correction filter includes a user-friendly tool for straightening images, but you can alter an image's perspective in all versions of Photoshop. Open Perspective.jpg from the CD and go to Edit > Transform > Perspective, or Image > Transform > Perspective in Elements (you'll need to unlock the file – see the sidebar). A box will appear around the image. To straighten the building's vertical lines drag the top-left handle to the left to increase the width at the top of the shot, then drag the bottom-left

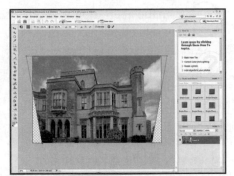

Straighten out a building's converging vertical walls using the Perspective Transform option in Photoshop and Elements

handle to the right. Click OK, and use the Crop Tool to remove the transparent areas from the corners.

Unlocking layers
When you open an image in Photoshop you'll see a locked padlock icon by the Background layer's thumbnail, which indicates that the image is locked. To alter an image's perspective using the Transform tools you need to unlock it. In Photoshop double-click the Background layer to unlock it and make it an image layer. Elements users will be prompted to unlock the layer by a dialog, and simply need to click OK.

THE LENS CORRECTION OPTION

Fix perspective distortion, and more, using CS2's versatile filter

To correct perspective distortion in CS2 open Perspective.jpg and go to Filter > Distort > Lens Correction. Drag the Vertical Perspective slider to -45 to make the vertical lines run parallel with the edges of the frame – and that's it! The filter has the edge over the Transform options because it also enables you fix the image's slight barrel distortion – drag the Remove Distortion slider to +3 to create perfectly perpendicular lines. If you have enough room around a building you can also use the Scale slider to get rid of the transparent areas the correction creates, instead of cropping the shot. Once you're happy with your correction click OK.

The Lens Correction filter enables you to straighten converging verticals and correct barrelling at the same time

Chromatic aberration

By-pass CS2's filter, and remove colour fringes from images using a more effective technique

Aberration.jpg
We've placed this image afflicted by chromatic aberration on the CD. If you have CS2 you can try removing the blue fringe using the Lens Correction filter's Chromatic Aberration slider, but you'll find it's not much cop. Then try the technique described in the box below – you should find that you enjoy more success.

Chromatic aberration is another lens-related artifact, which appears as blue or cyan fringes of colour that cling to the edges of high-contrast areas, and it's especially noticeable in shots taken with budget cameras, or camera phones. In our example shot, the dark branches against the bright sky suffer from blue fringing. CS2's Lens Correction filter includes a Chromatic Aberration slider that attempts to shift the colour fringes left or right to get rid of them, but it's almost impossible to get it to remove the

The Chromatic Aberration slider in the Lens Correction filter's interface can often make colour fringes look worse, rather than better!

fringes in our sample shot. However, there's a better method that can be used in any version of Photoshop.

HUE/SATURATION SOLUTION

Remove colour fringes effectively using an adjustment layer

You can use an adjustment layer to remove the blue fringes in our example shot – it's far more effective than using the Lens Correction filter. Add a Hue/Saturation adjustment layer, and in the dialog select Blues from the Edit menu. Reduce the Saturation of the blues to -59 to remove all traces of the colour fringe, while preserving the rest of the image's colours. This technique suits our sample image because it's mostly brown and green – there are no blue pixels in the scene apart from the unwanted fringes. If you do have blue in an image you'll need to select the fringe areas before adding the adjustment layer.

A quick tweak of the Hue/Saturation adjustment layer's Saturation slider is all it takes to remove colour fringes

Goodbye grain

The Reduce Noise filter lets you smooth-out grain while preserving important image detail

One of the most common image-spoiling artifacts you'll encounter is picture noise or grain. It can crop up in shots taken with a high ISO setting, and you can also spot grain in shots taken at night, especially in areas with a large expanse of graduated colour, such as skies. You might also encounter unsightly blocks of colour called 'jaggies', which are caused by high JPEG compression settings. The trick to removing these artifacts is to smooth-out an image's pixels without blurring important detail,

and you can do this effectively using the Reduce Noise filter in CS2 and Elements 3 and 4. Open the image Grain.jpg, go to Filter > Noise > Reduce Noise, and use the annotated screenshot below to guide you through the key components of the Reduce Noise filter. To reduce noise in pre-CS2 versions of Photoshop use the Magic Wand to select areas that are prone to noise (a dark sky, for example). Go to Filter > Noise > Median, and drag the Radius slider to the right to smooth-out grain and other artifacts, such as 'jaggies'.

ISO settings
When shooting in low light you can reduce the shutter speed to let more light into the camera for a better exposure. This minimises picture noise, but you'll need to use a tripod to avoid blurring. Alternatively, you can make your camera more sensitive to light, so that you can take a handheld shot at a faster shutter speed, by increasing the camera's ISO setting to 800 or even higher. However, higher ISO settings create 'noisier' shots.

MAKE LESS NOISE

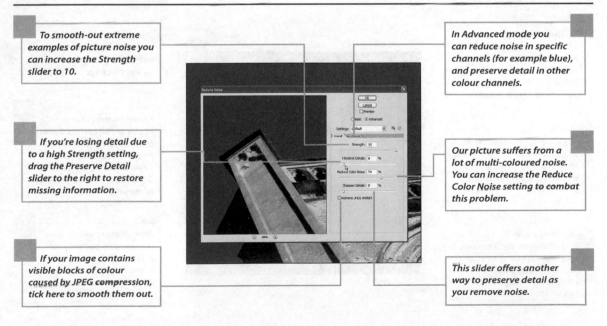

To smooth-out extreme examples of picture noise you can increase the Strength slider to 10.

In Advanced mode you can reduce noise in specific channels (for example blue), and preserve detail in other colour channels.

If you're losing detail due to a high Strength setting, drag the Preserve Detail slider to the right to restore missing information.

Our picture suffers from a lot of multi-coloured noise. You can increase the Reduce Color Noise setting to combat this problem.

If your image contains visible blocks of colour caused by JPEG compression, tick here to smooth them out.

This slider offers another way to preserve detail as you remove noise.

Adding artifacts

You can add artifacts to turn a digital image into a low-quality throw-away camera snap

This high-quality digital shot is artifact-free. We can 'rough it up', and give it more character, by adding a few artifacts

Colour uncoordinated
You can also enhance the cheap camera effect by experimenting with colour. Add a Hue/Saturation adjustment layer, and see how the image looks with over-saturated or under-saturated colours. This will help to make the image look like the product of a cheap and nasty camera, instead of a high-end digital SLR.

Throughout this chapter we've tackled various camera-induced artifacts to create noise-free, sharply focused versions of our photos, but now we're going to turn the science on its head, and create the effect of a shot riddled with camera artifacts. Filmmakers occasionally include footage shot on cheap 16mm cameras to add a 'documentary' feel to their film, and by faking the look of a print shot on a cheap camera we can give a digital picture a low-fi look. Cheap cameras tend to have low-quality lenses that cause vignetting and edge blurring – check out the screenshot below to see the artifacts we're going to recreate.

ARTIFICIAL ARTIFACTS

To fake the vignette effect you can get from a low-quality lens we'll show you how to darken the corners of the cropped shot.

Cheap cameras sometimes use square format negatives. We'll show you how to crop a landscape shot to create this effect.

A cheap plastic lens can lose focus towards its edges. This effect can be achieved using layers, filters and the Eraser Tool.

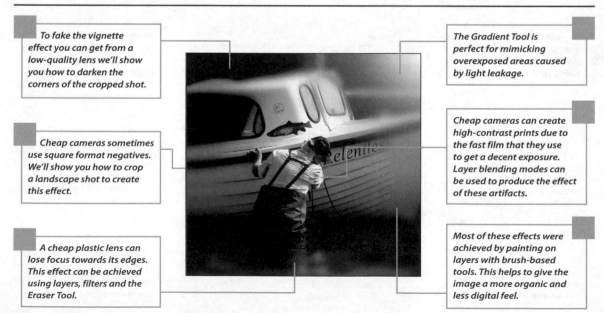

The Gradient Tool is perfect for mimicking overexposed areas caused by light leakage.

Cheap cameras can create high-contrast prints due to the fast film that they use to get a decent exposure. Layer blending modes can be used to produce the effect of these artifacts.

Most of these effects were achieved by painting on layers with brush-based tools. This helps to give the image a more organic and less digital feel.

Adding artifacts

Get medieval on a digital photo's pixels to
create a rough and ready, artifact-riddled print

1 Open Artifact.jpg from the CD. Some cheap plastic cameras create a square negative, so select the Crop Tool (C), hold down the [Shift] key to constrain the tool, and draw a square. Reposition the square so that the edges of the frame become greyed-out, and hit [Enter] to apply the crop.

2 Cheap cameras often use a high-speed film to capture sufficient light, and this can produce high-contrast shots. Duplicate the Background layer by dragging it on to the 'Create a new layer' button at the foot of the Layers palette. Set the layer's blending mode to Hard Light, and reduce the opacity of the layer a little to reduce the harshness of the contrast.

3 Go to Layer > Flatten Image to merge the two layers. Duplicate the merged layer, and with the copied layer targeted go to Filter > Blur > Gaussian Blur. Enter a high Radius setting of around 25, then use a soft-edged Eraser Tool to remove the blur from the centre of the shot, and leave the edges out of focus. This mimics the focal limitations of a cheap plastic lens.

4 Flatten the image again, then use the Burn Tool to darken the corners of the shot to create the type of vignetting effect associated with a cheap lens. To simulate an overexposed area caused by light leaking through the camera's casing create a new layer and draw a Foreground to Transparent Radial gradient, with the foreground colour set to white.

A touch of flare
You can add other artifacts to your shots by using filters such as Lens Flare (Filter > Render > Lens Flare). This mimics direct sunlight hitting the camera from the front, and illuminating the curved surface of the lens. The filter can produce a variety of effects, mimicking the types of flare you get from 35mm or Zoom lenses, for example.

Applying lens flare
Normally you have to apply a lens flare effect directly to your flattened image. You can't apply the filter to a transparent layer, and this means that once the lens flare has been added you can't move it around. You can get around this by filling a new layer with 50% grey, and applying the Lens Flare filter to this layer. If you change the layer's blending mode to Hard Light the grey will vanish, while the flare remains. You can now move the layer, and the effect, around.

PUTTING YOUR EDITING SKILLS INTO PRACTICE

We'll finish off by using many of the tools and techniques covered in this guide to edit some typical wedding photos, and create a stylish cover for a DVD photo album or slide show

The majority of this Focus Guide has been about helping you to choose the right tools and techniques to get your digital photos looking their best, and showing you how to use those tools. You should now be able to confidently brighten an underexposed photo, or rescue highlight detail from an overexposed shot, after analysing its histogram to see exactly where the problem areas are. As well as tackling tonal problems you should also be able to recognise colour problems and correct them by using tools such as the Photo Filter dialog to warm up a shot that has a cool colour cast. Photoshop and Elements give you a choice of several ways of doing most things, and by trying out a wide variety of tools you should hopefully have a feel for those that suit your particular way of working.

Getting creative

After going to the trouble of editing and enhancing your images there's no point leaving them sitting on your computer, and in this final chapter we'll return to many of the tools and techniques that we've covered in the previous six, and introduce a few new ones, as we turn a typical selection of wedding photos into a digital slide show. We'll start by making some basic tonal and colour

Page 112 *Rescue a shot by restoring important detail lost in the shadows*

Page 115 *Use one photo's healthy colours to remove casts from other shots*

Page 117 *Copy confetti from an image and add it to a different scene*

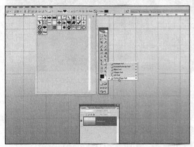

Page 119 *Use the Custom Shape Tool to design components for a DVD cover*

Page 119 *Use layer styles to make your 2D shapes stand out on the page*

Page 121 *Turn your photos into a slide show that you can email or burn to DVD*

corrections, using tools such as the Shadow/Highlight command, and also one we haven't looked at yet, Photoshop's Match Color command, which enables you to remove a colour cast from a series of images by applying the colour values from a correctly balanced shot to them. We'll also show you how to adapt the select and transform technique to add a shower of confetti to an image.

Then it's time to get seriously creative, as we show you how to create a cover for a photo DVD. You'll discover how to create a file with the correct dimensions, and how to use guides to help you with your design. We'll also show you how you can use features such as layer styles and symbols to add a creative flourish to your projects. With your cover complete, you'll obviously want something to go in it, and we'll show you how to compile your photos into a DVD slide show in Elements.

Make it personal!

All the files featured in this chapter are on the CD if you want to follow the various walkthroughs to the letter, but you can, of course, use your own images, particularly if you've got a stash of photos from a recent special occasion that you've been wondering what to do with!

Saving the day

Harness the power of Photoshop to rescue your imperfect reminders of a special occasion

Elements options
Elements 4 users can restore detail to this page's problem picture by using the Shadows/Highlights command, or by opening it in Quick Fix mode and using the Lighten Shadows slider to brighten the shadow areas without overexposing the highlights. See page 54 for more on both tools.

They say that time waits for no man, and this is certainly the case when you're trying to take photos at a special event. Weddings in particular seem to unfold at their own unstoppable speed; if you're not on the ball you can easily miss one-off photo opportunities, and you won't be popular if you keep asking people to pose for a retake because you've underexposed a shot or got the focus wrong! Fortunately, Photoshop can save the day by helping you to overcome a variety of problems, so before we create a

In this shot the groom and best man have strong shadows obscuring their eyes, due to harsh sunlight hitting them from the side

montage of wedding photos to adorn a DVD we'll make sure that each of our images is looking its best.

RESCUING SHADOW DETAIL

The Shadow/Highlight command selectively lightens the image

Open Groom.jpg. To avoid overexposing the subjects' white shirts, and burning-out highlight detail illuminated by direct sunlight, we set the camera to expose for the brightest objects in the scene, and this has left the areas obscured by shadow lacking in detail. Go to Image > Adjustments > Shadow/Highlight, and by default the tool will attempt to increase shadow detail. Drag the Shadows Amount slider to around 70% and you'll be able to capture the groom and best man's happy expressions. This shot now looks good enough to make a valuable contribution to a slideshow, wedding album or DVD cover montage.

The Shadow/Highlight command can restore detail lost in shadow, and reveal a great shot in the process

Blinded by the white

A well-composed shot can be ruined by blown highlights – here's how to restore missing detail

Most people hope that the sun shines on their wedding day, apart from the photographer that is! As most brides are covered from head to toe in white it can be very tricky to get a good shot of them without burning-out the finer detail adorning their expensive dresses, and a burst of flash is also liable to burn-out detail on the dress as it reflects off the garment. If you attempt to restore detail to burnt-out highlights you risk losing detail in the shadow and midtone areas, but fortunately the Shadow/Highlight

Direct sunlight, or a burst of flash, can burn-out important detail in the brightest highlights, especially if there's lots of white in the image

command is just as good at saving these kinds of shots, by applying its adjustments to specific tonal area.

Perfect preview

When you're adjusting the Shadow/Highlight sliders it's easy to forget what your original image looked like for reference. To see how your edited image compares with the original shot untick the Preview box – you should notice a dramatic improvement in highlight detail. If you go too far with your adjustment press [Alt]/[Option] to turn the Cancel button into a Reset button, and click this to start from scratch.

RESCUING HIGHLIGHT DETAIL

Tone things down using the additional Shadow/Highlight sliders

Open BrightBride.jpg, and go to Image > Adjustments > Shadow/Highlight (or Enhance > Adjust Lighting > Shadows/Highlights in Elements). By default the command will try to brighten shadows, so drag the Shadows Amount slider down to 0, and increase the Highlights Amount slider to 45%. To take more control over the adjustment tick the Show More Options box. Reduce the Tonal Width slider a little, to around 38%, to limit the changes to the brightest highlights and avoid altering correctly exposed shadows, and to improve detail in larger areas spoiled by burnt-out highlights increase the Radius slider to 58%.

As well as restoring lost detail, the Shadow/Highlight command also adds definition to the couple's faces

Staying sharp

Some photo opportunities are one-offs, so don't let poor focus spoil your important shots

Threshold slider
When you sharpen a shot it's easy to add artifacts to the image, and a high Amount setting combined with a large Radius value can cause highlights to burn-out. Reduce the combined effect of the Radius and Amount sliders by gently increasing the Threshold slider. The higher the Threshold value, the less effect the other sliders will have on the image.

When you're shooting at an event such as a wedding you get rare opportunities to capture large groups of friends and relatives in a single shot. Controlling a large crowd while attempting to set focus manually, can be a nightmare. You can set your camera to Auto Focus, which gives you one less thing to think about, but the camera can be confused by the moving crowd, causing images to come out blurred. We did get a sharper version of this shot, but it was a more conventional image, as the crowd weren't waving.

Shooting on Auto Focus, or moving the camera even slightly during a slow shutter exposure, can blur your images

We can use Photoshop's sharpening tools to rescue our more interesting, but technically flawed photos.

SHARPENING OPTIONS

Use Smart Sharpen or Unsharp Mask to wave goodbye to blurs

As we saw in Chapter 6, there are several ways to approach correcting a shot with focus problems. CS2's complex Smart Sharpen filter enables you to tackle different kinds of blur, such as lens blur or motion blur, and also lets you focus your editing on shadows or highlights to minimise sharpening artifacts. This particular group shot is slightly out of focus, but there's no problematic motion blur. This means you can use the simpler Unsharp Mask filter to improve the image. Using a less-complex tool can speed up your workflow, as you have fewer sliders to fiddle with. An Amount setting of 87% and a Radius of 3.4 pixels is enough to sharpen detail.

With many photo-fixing jobs less is more. The basic Unsharp Mask filter does a good job of rescuing this shot

Match Color

Use Photoshop's Match Color command to give a series of photos a consistent look

The Match Color command enables you to take a correctly colour-balanced shot and apply its colour values to other shots, so that they take on the same hues and tones. When you shoot an event like a wedding you'll want all your shots to have consistent colours, so that they'll look harmonious in an album or slide show. As the day goes by, however, lighting conditions can change – a sunny sky can cloud over, creating the danger of colour casts due to the changing temperature of the light, while flash light has a

The shot on the left is warm, while the image on the right has a cool tint – the Match Color command can make them consistent

different colour temperature to daylight, which can also make it tricky to capture consistent colours.

Vital statistics
Once you've found a source image that contains the colour information you need to alter problem shots you can save the Match Color settings for future use. In the Match Color dialog click Save Statistics. This will create an .sta file that records the source image you used, as well as settings such as Color Intensity. To colour-correct other shots open the Match Color dialog, click Load Statistics and target your saved file.

MATCH-MAKING

Quickly create a series of shots with a matching colour palette

Open CoolWedding.jpg. This shot of our bride has rather cold-looking blue whites, which make it clash with the warm look of other photos taken on the day. Open the healthier-looking shot of the groom, WarmWedding.jpg, then click on the cool shot to select it and go to Image > Adjustments > Match Color. Make sure the target file is CoolWedding.jpg, and the Source file is WarmWedding.jpg. The shot of the bride will be warmed up to match the warm colours in her husband's photo, and you can add more colour to her cheeks by pushing the Color Intensity slider to 123. The two shots will now sit happily side by side – which is just as well!

The Match Color command enables you to produce shots with consistent colours in seconds

Digital confetti

Use Photoshop's tools to digitally recreate scenes that you failed to capture on camera

Rapid fire!
As key events in weddings whiz past you can miss important shots, while photos you do take may be blurred. To capture more of the action (and avoid having to do extra photo-fixing) set your camera to rapid-fire mode. When you press the shutter many SLRs will take four or more shots in succession, making it more likely you'll get a better picture. Just make sure you have plenty of memory cards to store your shots on!

Anyone who has photographed a wedding will know how tricky it is to capture all the key events. Some of the action is easy to predict, such as the cutting of the cake, but another archetypal wedding shot is the happy couple being showered in confetti, and this isn't always easy to capture, as the snap on the right shows. We've been caught napping, and the confetti has been chucked before we had a chance to compose the shot; we've chopped off the groom's head, and caught the couple with their eyes

Our shot is poorly composed because we weren't on the ball when the confetti started flying – but we can find a use for the confetti!

shut. To create a more attractive image we'll open a different shot, and digitally add some confetti.

MIX AND MATCH

Take the best elements from two shots to create a perfect photo

Open WithConfetti.jpg, our poorly composed shot featuring lots of confetti. Open WithoutConfetti.jpg; this is a better composed shot, but there's barely a petal to be seen. On the facing page we'll show you how to transplant confetti from the first shot into the second to create a storm of petals. We'll use the Magic Wand Tool to isolate some petals, and copy them. After pasting them into the new shot a blur filter will add the effect of motion to the confetti (and smooth-out rough edges). We'll also turn a handful of petals into a storm with the help of the Transform tools, and as a finishing touch we'll tie the fake petals into the image by adding shadows.

This well-framed shot is a better portrayal of the happy couple – all it needs is some digital confetti

Compositing petals

Use the Magic Wand to select petals of confetti, and add them to the better-composed scene

1 Open the file WithConfetti.jpg. Select the Magic Wand Tool (W), and use it to select some confetti petals – see the sidebar for some selection tips. Edit > Copy your selected petals ([Ctrl]/[Command]+C). Open WithoutConfetti.jpg, and Edit > Paste the copied confetti ([Ctrl]/[Command]+V). The petals will appear on a new layer.

2 To double the amount of confetti select Paste again to add a second layer. Move this layer to offset it from the first one, and to make the petals look different go to Edit > Free Transform (or press [Ctrl]/[Command]+T. Hold down [Shift], and click and drag a corner handle to scale down the layer, and click and drag outside the layer to rotate it.

3 Hold down [Shift] and click the two confetti layer thumbnails in the layers palette to select them. Go to Layer > Merge Down, or Layer > Merge Layers in CS2 and Elements ([Ctrl]/[Command]+E), to create one combined layer of confetti. Go to Filter > Blur > Motion Blur. An Angle setting of 79 will make the confetti look like it's falling, and give it a softer edge. Set Distance to 31.

4 To add a shadow right-click ([Ctrl]-click) the confetti layer and choose Select Layer Transparency. The 'marching ants' will appear around the petals. Create a new layer, fill the selection with 50% grey, and set the blending mode to Color Burn. Place the shadow layer beneath the confetti layer, use the Move Tool to position the shadows over the couple, and scale them down a little.

Selection tips
The trick in step 1 is to select as much confetti as possible without selecting the background. If you find that you're selecting unwanted pixels tick the Contiguous box, so that you only select similar pixels that are adjacent to each other, and you'll be able to select individual petals. Hold down [Shift] and click to add more petals to the selection until you have enough to copy.

Move it
Use the Move Tool (V) to position the confetti and confetti shadow layers so that petals don't obscure key details, such as an eye or a smile. By adding confetti digitally you can control every petal, and create a perfectly composed shot. Use the Eraser Tool (E) to remove petals if necessary.

Create a DVD cover

With our image-editing finished we can start creating a stylish cover for our DVD album

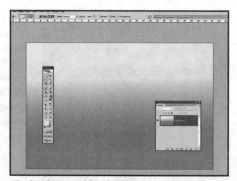

Pixel per inch

The more pixels you can cram into a square inch of image, the more detail you'll have to print. A pixels per inch (ppi) value of 300 is much better than the default value of 72, as it can present much more detail. The resolution of your PC's monitor is 72 dots per inch (dpi, which roughly equates to ppi). A 72ppi print would contain much less detail than a 300ppi version of the same image.

Y ou can use a host of extra Photoshop tools to help you present your images attractively, for example by adding text, symbols and other graphic design elements. On the next two pages we'll show you how to create a DVD cover to make your wedding slide show look more professional. You'll find a correctly sized DVD cover layout, called WeddingTemplate.psd, on the CD. To create a similar document from scratch go to File > New. Make the file 27.3cm wide and 18.3cm high, and set Resolution to 300 pixels per

The background for the DVD cover was created by drawing a linear gradient, using a pink sampled from the confetti in the photos

inch (see sidebar). Photoshop has lots of tools to help you design your layout, such as rulers and guides.

ADDED EXTRAS

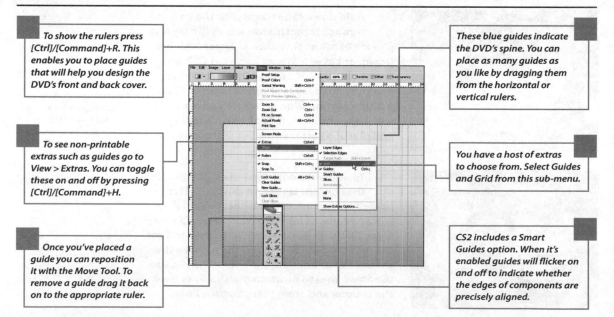

To show the rulers press [Ctrl]/[Command]+R. This enables you to place guides that will help you design the DVD's front and back cover.

To see non-printable extras such as guides go to View > Extras. You can toggle these on and off by pressing [Ctrl]/[Command]+H.

Once you've placed a guide you can reposition it with the Move Tool. To remove a guide drag it back on to the appropriate ruler.

These blue guides indicate the DVD's spine. You can place as many guides as you like by dragging them from the horizontal or vertical rulers.

You have a host of extras to choose from. Select Guides and Grid from this sub-menu.

CS2 includes a Smart Guides option. When it's enabled guides will flicker on and off to indicate whether the edges of components are precisely aligned.

Creating shapes

Put Photoshop's vector-based symbols and shapes to good use to enhance your design

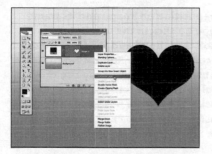

1 The first thing to do is create some shapes to frame the edited wedding photos. Go to the toolbox, and click and hold on the Rectangle Tool's compartment to see the full list of tools. Select the Custom Shape Tool, go to the options bar and click the button next to the Shape preview to open the Custom Shape picker. Select Heart Card from the default set (see sidebar).

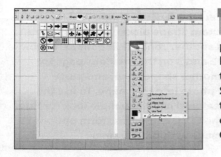

2 Click the 'Shape layers' button in the options bar. Press [Shift] to constrain the shape's proportions, and draw a heart shape on the front of the cover. This creates a new layer containing a vector shape. Go to the Layers palette, right-click ([Ctrl]-click) the layer, and choose Rasterize Layer to covert the vector shape to a bitmap image that you can edit in the same way as a photo.

3 Open one of the wedding shots. Go to Select > All, and copy it. Use the Magic Wand Tool to select the heart shape and go to Edit > Paste Into. This will create a new layer with a photo inside a heart-shaped mask. To scale the photo down inside the heart target the new layer and choose Edit > Transform > Scale. Hide the original heart layer for the moment (click the eye icon).

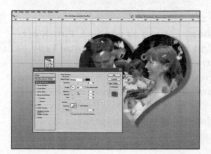

4 To make the heart-shaped photo frame look like a piece of floating confetti click the 'Add a layer style' icon in the Layers palette and choose Drop Shadow from the list. Experiment with the Distance, Spread and Size sliders to make the shape stand out from the background, and reduce the shadow's opacity to 45% to make it more subtle. Click OK to apply the layer style.

Loading shapes
If you can't see a particular shape in the Custom Shape picker you'll need to load its set by clicking the arrow at the top-right of the palette and selecting the set from the menu. The shapes we're using are from the default set, and you'll also find them in the Shapes set. When you draw your shape it will be filled with the foreground colour; make sure this is set to black so that you can select the shape easily with the Magic Wand in step 3.

Shapes in Elements
If you're using Elements you'll need to OK the dialog asking you to simplify the shape layer before using the Magic Wand Tool; this has the same effect as the Rasterize command in Photoshop. You can add a drop shadow to the heart shape in Elements by going to the Styles and Effects palette. Click on the menu at the top-left of the palette and choose Layer Styles, then choose Drop Shadows from the menu on the right. Target the heart layer in the Layers palette, and click on one of the drop shadow presets to apply the effect.

Completing your cover

Adapt the techniques featured on the previous page to insert more photos into confetti shapes

Spine image
You can create a quick confetti-shaped frame to adorn the DVD's spine by duplicating an existing frame that you created for the cover. Drag a confetti-shaped frame's layer thumbnail on to the 'Create a new layer' icon. This will duplicate the contents of the selected layer, as well as any layer styles associated with that layer. You can then scale down the layer to a suitable size.

Do it your way...
You can adapt the tips and techniques featured in this chapter to create a DVD or poster design based on any theme. You should also have all the skills required to overcome colour, tone, focus and composition problems, and create photos that are fit for a high-quality design.

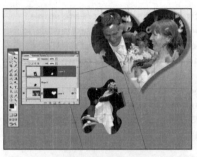

5 Select the Custom Shape Tool, open the Custom Shape picker and select Blob 1, which is another confetti-like shape. Follow steps 1, 2 and 3 on the previous page to create another shape layer, and paste another photo into the shape. To use the image featured in our example look for Hug.jpg on the CD. Use the Transform options to fit the image within the frame.

6 To reposition an image and its frame in one go click in the gap between the photo's thumbnail and the layer mask. A chain icon will appear, indicating that they're now linked, and you can use the Move Tool to drag the confetti shape and the image inside it to a new position. You can also transform the shape and its contents using the Edit > Transform options.

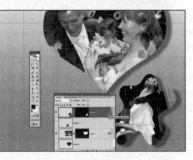

7 To quickly add a drop shadow to the new shape in CS2 and Elements hold down [Alt]/[Option] and drag the effect icon (the small 'f') from the heart layer to the blob layer to apply the same style to that layer. In other versions you'll need to click the effect name or icon below the layer thumbnail, and drag them on to the dividing line below the target layer.

8 You can now add as many other photos to shape frames as you like. Finish off your design by using the Horizontal Type Tool (T) to add some text. Use the Eyedropper Tool (I) to sample the pink from the bottom of the cover's gradient texture to colour the text, and make the text stand out by adding a drop shadow layer style.

Create a slide show

Elements 4 has all you need to create a slide show of your images to email or burn to DVD

Once you've polished up the photos from your own special occasion, and designed a DVD cover, you can copy your photos on to a disc and present it as a wedding or birthday gift, or just hand out copies to friends and family. If you own Elements 4 you can go one step further, and create an all-singing, all-dancing slide show that you can burn to DVD. The images can be linked together with a variety of slick transitions and other effects, and the whole slide show can unfold to a backing track of suitable music,

You can turn any collection of photos into an entertaining slide show with ease using Elements 4's Create feature

or a commentary, ensuring that your image-editing and design work is seen by the widest-possible audience!

Share and enjoy
An alternative way to share your photos is to use Elements' Slide Show Output window to create an email-friendly slide show. You can convert it into a small .wmv movie that will play on other PCs, or even a convert it to a PDF at the click of a button. If you have the full version of Photoshop and want to create slide shows it's worth spending £60 on Elements 4, as it has enough unique tools to make it a powerful complementary program.

MOVING PICTURES

Compile a slide show complete with visual effects and sound

To turn a folder of photos into a slide show click the Create icon at the top of the Elements 4 workspace. This opens the Organizer, and the Creation Setup window. Choose Slide Show and click OK. Use the Slide Show Preferences window to select the default transitions, and then adjust the time each shot should remain on-screen. You can choose to apply a pan and zoom to all slides, or keep them static. Click OK to open the Slide Show Editor. You can fine-tune the slide show by changing certain transitions manually, and even add text and a voiceover. When you're happy with the preview click Output and choose Burn to Disc.

Arrange your photos on a timeline, and add a range of effects, to create a stunning slide show

On your CD

Here's how to get the most from the packed disc that accompanies your Focus Guide

Featured resources

- ☐ **Serif DrawPlus 5.0** (PC only, full version)
- ☐ **50 royalty-free images from iStockphoto**
- ☐ **Exclusive video tutorials**
- ☐ **Full 'Brushes & Painting' Focus Guide in PDF form** (Issue 24)
- ☐ **All the source files you need to complete the walkthroughs**

To access the resources and files on this disc, including the iStockphoto collection of images and exclusive video tutorials, first insert the CD into your drive. Whether you're using a Mac or a Windows PC, the disc will work equally well. If the disc interface doesn't run automatically, look at the opposite page to find out how to start your installation manually.

Before you go on
The first item that should appear on your screen is the disclaimer

window: here you'll need to click on 'I Accept'. Please remember that this disc has been scanned and tested at all stages of production, but – as with all new software – we still recommend that you run a virus checker before use. We also recommend that you have an up-to date backup of your hard disk before using this disc. Future Publishing does not accept responsibility for any disruption, damage and/or loss to your data or computer system that may occur while using this disc, or the data and programs on it.

SERIF DRAWPLUS 5.0 (FULL VERSION)

A complete drawing, graphics and illustration package for the PC

With this full version of Serif's DrawPlus 5.0 you'll soon be using the power of scalable vector graphics to create logos, full-page illustrations, animated web graphics and more. This complete drawing, graphics and illustration package fulfils all your creative needs, whether you're an experienced user taking advantage of the full range of tools on offer, or a beginner using the built-in Wizards facility to help you learn as you go. Use DrawPlus to create stunning original artwork, or simply take advantage of the integral design tools and get immediate results.

Create eye-catching logos, striking illustrations and stunning web graphics with this full version of Serif's DrawPlus

www.serif.com

PFG41
ON YOUR CD

Serif Draw Plus 5.0 (PC full version)
50 royalty-free images from iStockphoto
Exclusive video tutorials
Full 'Brushes & Painting'
Focus Guide in PDF form

Photoshop

Please consult your network administrator before attempting to install software on a networked PC.

Installation

Once the CD is running you'll see a range of options in the menu bar. Click on a link to access the section that you require. Some files may need to be extracted from a Zip archive; try using WinZip (**www.winzip.com**) to do this if your version of Windows doesn't have a de-archiving utility. Our video tutorials need the latest QuickTime Player, from **www.apple.com/quicktime/download**. If you have a query about your disc then you can email **support@futurenet.co.uk** for help. To talk to a member of the team, call **01225 822743**. We can only provide basic advice on using the disc interface and installing the supplied software. We cannot give in-depth help on specific programs, or on your system configuration.

Starting your installation manually
PC users: click on the Windows Start button and click Run. Then click Browse and go to the CD directory in My Computer. Look for a file called PSFGi.exe and double-click it. Then click OK in the Run dialogue, and the disc should then load up. Mac users: Double-click the disc icon, then double-click PFGi-OSX to launch the interface.

EXCLUSIVE VIDEO TUTORIALS

Improve your Photoshop skills with the help of our resident guru

Discover how to wield Photoshop's tools like a master with the help of George Cairns, the author of this Focus Guide. George will take you through many of the walkthroughs featured in this guide, so you can see at first hand how to use Photoshop's tools to correct and enhance your images. The tutorials cover everything from using the Clone Stamp to remove unwanted elements from photos to combining images with different exposures to create a perfect shot. The tutorials have been created in the QuickTime format. Make sure you have the latest free version of the QuickTime Player by visiting the URL below.

Our exclusive videos show you how to get the most from Photoshop's powerful and versatile toolset

www.apple.com/quicktime

50 royalty-free images

These top-quality images from iStockphoto will add a professional touch to your projects

50 great images!
On the CD you'll find these four images and a lot more in medium-resolution JPEG format. To see the full range and make purchases, visit **www.istockphoto.com**. The images on your disc are strictly not for resale.

This selection of 50 images is worth over $150, and is an incredible sample of what iStockphoto has to offer. The iStockphoto library contains over a million images, and 7,000 new shots are added every week. Each image is reviewed for quality and legal integrity by a worldwide network of highly-qualified inspectors.

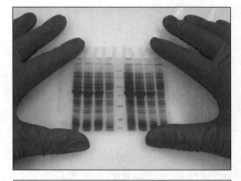

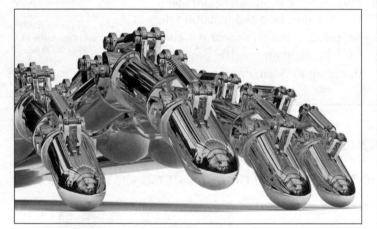

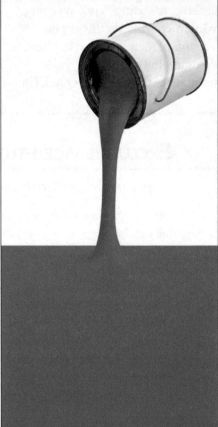

Adobe Photoshop Special Effects

PLUS
SECOND FULL
FOCUS GUIDE
ON DISC

☐ Discover how to transform the photos that you take every day with a range of stunning photo-realistic makeovers, including solarization, film noir, high-fashion and Lomo effects

☐ 100% exclusive tutorials – the ORIGINAL monthly Photoshop guide, with all the know-how you need

☐ 232 pages of expert Photoshop information in the FocusGuide and on the accompanying CD-ROM

Includes a packed disc with full programs, tools and extras, exclusive video tutorials, a COMPLETE second Focus Guide in PDF format, all the files you need to complete the tutorials, and much more!

All contents subject to change

Glossary

We always try to minimise the jargon, but it helps to add a few words of Photoshop-speak to your vocabulary…

Anti-aliasing
Moving pixels around can cause undesirable jagged edges to appear, where edited pixels have not blended smoothly together. Anti-aliasing refers to the process of smoothing out these jagged edges for a more natural look.

Blending modes
Blending modes are used to determine how the pixels in a layer are blended with underlying pixels on other layers. By applying specific blending modes to individual layers, you can create a wide variety of effects.

Brushes
Brushes enable you to paint on Photoshop images with colour, pixels from other images and predefined patterns. They mimic real brushes in that you can alter their size, hardness and texture.

Calibration
The process of adjusting a device to bring its behaviour into line with a known specification, helping to reproduce colours accurately. For example, colour monitors are calibrated to a specific colour temperature, gamma, and black-and-white luminance.

Colour channels
There are three or more colour channels in all full-colour images, depending on which colour mode you're using. RGB mode contains red, green and blue channels, while CMYK mode has cyan, magenta, yellow and black channels.

DNG
Digital Negative, a publicly available archival format for the Raw files generated by digital cameras that has been developed by Adobe, and which is supported by a wide range of camera and software manufacturers.

Filters
A filter is a preset tool within Photoshop which applies an effect to an image. Some filters apply their effect in one click, while others offer more complex settings. Filter categories include Sharpen, Blur, Artistic and Stylize. Each of these offers further options via fly-out menus.

Gamut
The range of colour that a device (such as a printer) can produce, or the range of colour that a colour model can represent. If a colour is said to be 'out of gamut', it will not be reproduced accurately by the printing process or other intended destination.

GIF (or .gif)
A type of image file format best suited to producing simple images for the web. Examples include logos, buttons and anything made up of just a few flat colours.

Greyscale
An image is greyscale if it contains no colour information. Using Photoshop, you can transform a colour image into black-and-white, with many gradations of grey, in a single channel.

JPEG (or .jpeg)
A type of image file format that gives a desirable combination of small file size and good-quality photo reproduction. It's commonly used in digital cameras to store the images that you take. The small file sizes also make it ideal for the web.

Layers
Layers containing effects or elements of images can be stacked on top of the original image layer (the Background) in order to change the appearance of the image or create composite images. Layers do not directly affect the layers beneath them, just as a blurry piece of glass placed over a photograph does not actually affect the photograph; in both cases, it's the appearance that has been changed, with the original image left unaltered.

Marquee
The flashing dotted outline that surrounds a selection. You'll also see it referred to in some places as 'marching ants'.

Pixel
An abbreviation for 'picture element', it's essentially a tiny dot of colour on screen. Most images are made of up of millions of pixels, which combine to make an image look seamless. Zoom in very close to an image, however, or enlarge it to a high degree, and you can clearly see these individual pixels.

PSD (or .psd)
Adobe Photoshop's own file format, which preserves elements such as layers and channels. If you're editing an image file, it's sensible to save it as a .psd, in order for the changes you've made to remain editable when you next open it.

Rasterising
When you 'rasterise' a graphical element, you convert it from a vector to a pixel-based image. It will no longer be scalable like a vector, but can still be edited, like other images in Photoshop.

Raw file
Raw files are unprocessed image files generated by digital cameras that support the format. Rather than being processed 'in-camera', the data is left uncompressed and unedited until it's opened in an editing program such as Photoshop using the Adobe Camera Raw plug-in.

Resolution
A measure of how many pixels make up an image. A resolution of 300ppi (pixels per inch) is widely regarded as the minimum if you're intending to print your images. 72ppi is sufficient for images intended for the web.

Selection
Any part of an image which you select with Photoshop's tools, usually indicated by a marquee around it. Making selections enables you to work on parts of an image, or remove them, without affecting the rest of the image.

Thumbnail
A small, 'thumbnail-sized' version of an image. You'll find them in folders of images and in Photoshop's File Browser. Because they're smaller than a full-size image they're fast to load, and you can browse through them more quickly, which makes finding the file you're after much easier.

Tool options bar
When a tool is selected, the corresponding tool options bar automatically appears along the top of the Photoshop window, giving you access to various options relating specifically to that tool. These often include effects such as anti-aliasing and feathering.

Index

Turn straight to the information you need
with the help of our comprehensive index